An account of The Fifth International Forum
November 1974

compiled by
Jack McGill

Investing in Scotland

Published for the
International Forum of the Scottish Council
(Development and Industry)

Collins Glasgow and London

ISBN 0 00 460119 10
© International Forum 1975
Scottish Council (Development and Industry)
Printed in Great Britain
set in Baskerville

Contents

Participants in the Forum

Professor K. J. W. Alexander,
Head, Department of Economics,
Strathclyde University

L. B. Aitken,
Industrial Director,
Scottish Council (Development &
Industry)

J. Anderson,
Chairman, Central Regional Council

W. M. Adams,
Aberdeen Manager,
Scottish Council (Development &
Industry)

Mrs. Jean Balfour,
Chairman, Countryside Commission
for Scotland

Lord Balfour of Burleigh,
Director, Bank of Scotland,
Chairman, Scottish Arts Council

H. A. Ballantyne,
Sir Robert McAlpine & Sons Ltd.

I. H. Stuart Black,
Chairman, General Accident Fire &
Life Assurance Corporation Ltd.

J. O. Blair-Cunynghame,
Chairman, National & Commercial
Banking Group

John M. Boyd,
Executive Councillor (Scotland),
Amalgamated Union of Engineering
Workers

David T. A. Boyle,
Director and Manager,
Morgan Grenfell (Scotland) Ltd.

John S. Boyle,
Director, External Relations,
Scottish Council (Development &
Industry)

Dr. Lawrence Boyle,
Chief Executive,
Strathclyde Regional Council

A. J. Brooke,
Glasgow Manager,
Scottish Council (Development &
Industry)

Hon. Bernard Bruce,
Partner, Stirling & Co.

5

Hon. James Bruce,
Member of National Board,
Scottish Woodland Owners' Assoc.

Dr. G. M. Burnett,
Principal & Vice-Chancellor,
Heriot-Watt University

V. Camacho,
Director, Scottish Airports,
British Airports Authority

Howard Cape,
National Association of Local
Government Officers

D. Carmichael,
Society of Post Office Executives

C. G. Carnie,
Partner, Crouch & Hogg

A. D. Chisholm,
Manager, Bredero (Scotland)

J. R. Clarke,
Director of Education, Aberdeen

Lord Clydesmuir,
Chairman of Executive,
Scottish Council (Development &
Industry)

W. D. Coats,
Director, Coats Patons Ltd.

David J. Cobbett,
General Manager,
British Railways, Scottish Region

F. M. Cook,
Managing Director,
B.P. Refinery (Grangemouth) Ltd.

James R. Cowan,
Director, National Coal Board,
Scottish Area

A. Y. W. Cowie,
Director for Scotland,
Department of Employment

W. R. Crooke,
Society of Post Office Executives

Alastair U. Cross,
Lord Provost of Perth

James Currie,
Currie Shipping Lines

J. L. Daniaud,
London Manager,
Total Oil Marine Ltd.

W. H. Davidson,
Business Development Manager
(Energy)
The Royal Bank of Scotland Ltd.

Colonel F. T. Davies,
International Forum Committee,
Scottish Council (Development &
Industry)

Dr. W. J. Lyon Dean,
Chairman, Herring Industry Board

W. C. Dewar,
General Manager,
Clydesdale Bank Ltd.

Emil Dietlicher,
Deputy Vice-President,
Swiss Bank Corporation

Alexander Dunbar,
Director, Scottish Arts Council

Rear Admiral
D. A. Dunbar-Nasmith,
Deputy Chairman,
Highlands & Islands Development
Board

The Earl of Dunmore,
Director,
Charles Barker Scotland Ltd.

Colin R. Dunn,
Director,
Scottish Council Research Institute

A. D. Eaton,
Projects Director,
Motherwell Bridge Engineering Ltd.

Gerald H. Elliot,
Vice-Chairman,
Christian Salvesen (Managers) Ltd.

Russell Fairgrieve, MP
Scottish Conservatives Members'
Committee

Andrew Forman,
Divisional Officer,
U.S.D.A.W.

R. Mayson Foster,
Area Vice-President,
Gulf Oil European Co.

Robert E. Fox,
Managing Director,
Oil Exploration (Holdings) Ltd.

Bishop Michael Foylan,
Bishop of Aberdeen

James Gallagher,
District Organiser and Chairman,
Scottish Council of the
Union of Post Office Workers

R. H. Gardiner,
Financial Director,
Brown Brothers & Co. Ltd.

J. L. Garthwaite,
Director,
Stenhouse Scotland Ltd.

J. P. Gibson,
Director, Offshore Supplies Office,
Department of Energy

Sir Andrew Gilchrist,
Chairman,
Highlands & Islands Development
Board

P. A. Gillibrand,
Director, British Airways Scotland

S. Gooding,
Provost of Stevenson,
Chairman, Scottish Regional
Committee, T.&.G.W.U.

Major P. Hunter Gordon,
Chairman, A.I. Welders Ltd.

L. M. Harper Gow,
Chairman, Christian Salvesen Ltd.

Iain E. Graham,
Managing Director,
Howden Compressors Ltd.

Sir William S. Gray,
Lord Provost of Glasgow

W. Gregson,
Assistant General Manager,
Ferranti Ltd.

Sir Douglas Haddow,
Chairman, North of Scotland
Hydro Electric Board

7

A. S. Halford-MacLeod,
Adviser, Foreign Affairs &
Physical Distribution
Scottish Council (Development &
Industry)

John K. Hall,
Chairman,
Aberdeen Construction Group Ltd.

F. R. C. Hamilton,
Society of Post Office Executives

J. N. Harley,
Regional General Manager,
The Royal Bank of Scotland Ltd.

Douglas Henderson, MP,
Scottish National Party

Cyril Herring,
Chief Executive, Regional Division,
British Airways

Professor F. G. T. Holliday,
Acting Principal,
University of Stirling

I. E. F. Hope,
Director, Stenhouse Scotland Ltd.

J. D. H. Hume,
Managing Director,
Howden Group Ltd.

James Jack,
General Secretary
Scottish Trades Unions Congress

Peter Jay,
Economics Editor, The Times

Rev. W. B. Johnston,
Convener, Church & Nations
Committee, Church of Scotland

David Kelly,
P.A. Management Consultants Ltd.

Professor J. A. Kennerley,
Director,
Strathclyde Business School

Robin S. N. Lane,
Financial Director,
Glenlivet Distillers Ltd.

H. W. Laughland,
Managing Director,
Scottish Aviation Ltd.

Sir Donald R. Liddle,
Chairman,
Cumbernauld Development
Corporation

Sir William J. Lithgow, BT,
Vice-Chairman, Scott-Lithgow Ltd.

G. G. McAndrew,
Group Planning Manager,
Sidlaw Industries Ltd.

D. M. McCallum,
Director & General Manager,
Ferranti Ltd.

Dr. R. G. L. McCrone,
Under-Secretary and Chief Economic
Adviser,
Scottish Economic Planning Dept.

D. McDonald,
Chairman & Chief Executive,
Parsons Peebles Industries Ltd.

D. G. MacDonald,
Managing Director,
John Menzies (Holdings) Ltd.

Raymond Macdonald,
Scottish Secretary, T.&.G.W.U.

Jack McGill,
Chief Executive, Scotsource

T. McGregor,
*Chairman, South East of Scotland
Development Authority*

W. Mackenzie,
*Political Director,
Scottish Liberal Party*

W. P. G. Maclachlan,
*Personnel Director,
Burmah Oil Company Ltd.*

Robin McLellan,
Chairman, Scottish Tourist Board

Maitland Mackie,
*Chairman, North East of Scotland
Development Authority*

Alex Mair,
*Director & Chief Executive,
Grampian Television Ltd.*

P. M. Mansfield,
*Controller, Planning,
Scottish Postal Board*

J. D. Marquis,
*Managing Director,
Irvine Development Corporation*

John Matheson,
*Past President STUC
and Divisional Officer NUR*

Alfred Matter,
*Head, Economic Research Dept.,
Swiss Bank Corporation*

A. M. Mearns,
*Divisional Manager,
Burroughs Machines Ltd.*

Bruce Millan, MP,
Minister of State, Scottish Office

I. A. Duncan Millar,
*Chairman,
Tayside Regional Council*

Hugh Moran,
*Director, Scotland West Industrial
Promotion Group*

Michael J. Moran,
*Managing Director,
Microwave & Electronic Systems
Ltd.*

H. R. Morrison,
*Inverness Manager, Scottish Council
(Development & Industry)*

Sir Nicholas G. Morrison,
*Permanent Under-Secretary of State
Scottish Office*

A. M. Mowat,
*Group Personnel Manager,
Scottish & Newcastle Breweries
Ltd.*

W. A. Gordon Muir,
*Chairman, Scottish Special Housing
Association*

J. Munro,
Acting Editor, Glasgow Herald

R. H. Murdoch,
*Marketing Director,
National Coal Board, Scottish Area*

H. E. H. Murphy,
*Regional Director,
Automobile Association*

9

Alexander F. Mutch,
Chairman,
Grampian Regional Council

H. W. J. Nash,
Burmah Oil Co. Ltd.

E. R. Nixon,
Managing Director,
IBM United Kingdom Ltd.

Professor Peter R. Odell,
Director,
Economic Geography Institute,
Netherlands School of Economics

M. J. Parker,
Director, Central Planning Unit,
National Coal Board

John A. D. Paton,
Member London Executive,
Scottish Council (Development &
Industry)

Lord Polwarth

W. S. Quaile,
Chairman,
The Stock Exchange – Scottish

J. W. Rasmussen,
Special Adviser on Oil Related
Activities, Scottish Council
(Development & Industry)

B. A. Reamsbottom,
The Civil & Public Services
Association

L. C. Roberts,
Department of Trade & Industry

L. F. Robertson,
Deputy Chairman & Chief
Executive
Grampian Holdings Ltd.

P. M. Robertson,
President, Association of County
Councils in Scotland

W. N. Robertson,
Assistant General Manager
(Overseas)
General Accident Fire & Life
Assurance Corporation Ltd.

Dr. W. S. Robertson,
Executive Vice-President,
Scottish Council (Development &
Industry)

James Saunders,
Manager International Forum,
Scottish Council (Development &
Industry)

R. Scott,
Bank of Scotland

R. I. Shanks,
Director of Industrial Development,
South East of Scotland Development
Authority

Rev. Geoffrey M. Shaw,
Convener,
Strathclyde Regional Council

John F. Smith,
Lord Provost of Aberdeen

Professor R. A. Smith,
formerly Principal,
Heriot-Watt University

C. J. Steer,
Marketing Services Manager,
Plessey Co. Ltd.

Professor Sir Frederick Stewart,
*Professor of Geology, Edinburgh
University. Chairman, Advisory
Board for Research Councils*

Graham R. Strachan,
*Managing Director,
John Brown Engineering
(Clydebank) Ltd.*

Lord Taylor of Gryfe,
*Chairman,
British Railways (Scottish) Board*

Sir Patrick M. Thomas,
Chairman, Scottish Transport Group

James Thomson,
*General Manager,
Edinburgh Savings Bank*

Francis L. Tombs,
*Chairman, South East of Scotland
Electricity Board*

Sir John Toothill,
Director, Ferranti Ltd.

Peter H. J. de Vink,
Director, Ivory & Sime

W. P. Walker,
*President,
Edinburgh Chamber of Commerce*

Derek A. Webster,
*Chairman & Editorial Director,
Scottish Daily Record and Sunday
Mail Ltd.*

J. C. Williamson,
*North East Area Chairman,
Scottish Council (Development &
Industry)*

Dr. Neville F. Woodward,
*Chairman,
Forth Technical Services Ltd.*

Sir William McEwan Younger,
*Chairman International Forum,
Scottish Council (Development &
Industry)*

Foreword

This book contains the report of our Fifth International Forum, again compiled by Jack McGill, and I am delighted to introduce it to you with this brief Foreword.

We felt the theme "Investing in Scotland's Future" to be a timely one, indeed an urgent one, because even in this depressed economic climate there is no doubt that we should be looking to what our investment priorities must be if we are to realise the full benefits of all our resources, notably North Sea oil. With the pace and scale of developments in Scotland, choices clearly have to be made. The knowledge that the resources are there has created a new mood of confidence in Scotland, particularly in the field of public investment which can no longer be looked upon as a hand-out from central government.

One of the most important roles of the Scottish Council is to help form public opinion particularly on issues, such as these, which are crucial to the economic and social well-being of everyone who lives and works in Scotland.

Five years ago the International Forum was set up to help identify the factors which could become the major influences of our future, and provide an opportunity for debating them in an informal atmosphere in which people with interests in all aspects of the life of Scotland, and with the power to influence events, could be brought together.

Since that time the Forum has become an established and important event in the Scottish calendar. This is reflected also in the interest shown in it by those who represent the press, radio and television.

The reader of this book will find from the calibre of the speakers, and the quality of the debate at the Forum, evidence of the concern of all who took part to ensure that we make the right decisions for the benefit of Scotland and thereby the United Kingdom as a whole. *Clydesmuir*

Introduction

The Fifth International Forum, sponsored by the Scottish Council (Development and Industry), was held at Aviemore, Inverness-shire, on November 6th and 7th, 1974. Like the previous International Forums it attracted to it academics, accountants, agriculturalists, artists, bankers, broadcasters, churchmen, economists, industrialists, journalists, lawyers, politicians and trades unionists – 150 from the broad spectrum of Scottish life, British institutions, and some representing organisations in Continental Europe and the United States. They were there to listen and react to the various speakers who before the conference began had submitted papers.

As Lord Clydesmuir, chairman of the Scottish Council, said at the outset of the discussions: "The benefit of the Forum is in carrying new ideas forward through the influence that each wields in their own particular sphere of activity thereby getting action where it can count, rather than attempting to reach a concensus opinion . . . it (the Forum) is not meant just to be a question and answer session, that is why it is set up in a way so as to try and promote the exchange of opinions between the participants and the speakers . . ."

The *raison d'être* of the International Forum is ". . . to expose Scotland to the influence of the changes taking place throughout the world. It is not expected to reach conclusions thereby. Action – except within individual spheres of influence of participants – is not one of the purposes of the International Forum, but if a direction is pointed this will undoubtedly be taken up . . ."

15

Though that, indeed, remains true, the developments which are taking place in Scotland on the economic front through North Sea oil, about which Professor Peter Odell, Professor of Economic Geography at Erasmus University, Rotterdam, made some startling predictions, and politically with the setting up of a Scottish Assembly – an elected body which will possibly after 1977 make the decisions which are important to the future of the Scottish people – the world is, perhaps, being exposed to the influence of changes taking place in Scotland.

Certainly in Western Europe it is the one place where the economic and political changes taking place are the most dramatic. The changes are worthy of the attention of students of economics and politics.

The reason for this book is to provide a much wider audience, both inside and outside Scotland, with an insight into the thinking of those people who helped to influence and formulate policies. It also shows the dissension and argument which take place when a nation attempts to sort out its priorities for the future. The basic question is how best can they be achieved. What kind of investment is required, and what size of investment is necessary?

The material forming the basis of the book, like its predecessor last year, *Scotland's Goals*, has been taken from the papers presented by the various speakers and the discussion which took place during the two days the Forum was held. For the purposes of continuity the sequence of the contributions has been occasionally rearranged, but not, it is hoped, placed out of context. Minor changes were made to some of the contributions and a certain amount of editing of the discussions has taken place. Additions have been made by way of explanation. The chapter of Conclusions is the opinion of the compiler about what was achieved, or otherwise, and it is accepted that it might not correspond to the opinion held by any one of those who took part.

Certain developments have taken place since the Forum was held and these, where possible, have been included. But it is recognised that certain events – mainly political decisions – will take place by the time the book is published. To the knowledge of the compiler such events will not radically alter the views put forward in the book.

It has become clear that the International Forum has achieved a status of its own. The people who took part obviously felt confident that their views could be exchanged in an atmosphere which was wholly constructive. Perhaps a measure of the success of the Forum was that it was greatly over-subscribed within weeks of it being known when it would be held. Perhaps another indication of its importance was the fact that none of the participants succumbed to the temptation of enjoying the delights of the surrounding area during the two days.

Michael Fry, Economics Correspondent of the *Scotsman* newspaper, wrote of it: "One optimistic Scottish Council man told me that he looked forward to the International Forum becoming as integral a part of the Scottish calendar as the General Assembly or the Mod. The 1974 Forum, which took place at Aviemore, looks in retrospect as if it could well have been a major step towards achieving that ambition. Indeed, it produced an event which may one day count as historic . . .

"The 1974 International Forum may have marked a turning-point in the thinking about the Scottish economy – the point where it dawned on people both at home and abroad that the wealth and opportunities that flow from the North Sea will exceed what even the wildest optimists ever dared hope or imagine."

The International Forum wishes to acknowledge the support by grants of Grampian Television Limited, the Scottish International Education Trust, and the Scottish Daily Record Limited.

The compiler wishes to acknowledge the secretarial assistance of Miss Susan Campbell of Scotsource and Miss Iris Leitch of International Forum. Acknowledgment of sources of information is made throughout the book.

> J.M.
> *Edinburgh January 1975*

chapter 1

World
Economy

The world economy faces twin perils. Sharp recession and raging inflation. Recovery from both will take considerable time, with a large number of changes occurring over the next five to ten years. The inevitability of the situation is not in question – the same discussions are being heard in London, Brussels, Paris, Geneva, Munich, New York and Edinburgh. The degree to which either recession, or inflation, or both, affects a particular country or region is a matter of debate amongst politicians, economists and financiers. Various reasons or combinations of reasons are given for the state of affairs in the capitalist economies, a state of affairs which is not selective and which is not confining itself to those countries which have a mixed mixed/capitalist capitalist economy.

Two views, not necessarily conflicting, were put forward at the International Forum – one by Peter Jay, Economics Editor of *The Times* newspaper, and the other by Alfred Matter, head of the Economics Research Department of the Swiss Bank Corporation.

According to Jay, the world's balance of payments have been knocked totally off balance for the forseeable future by the huge rise in oil prices in the winter of 1973/74, coupled with the inability or unwillingness of the oil-producing countries to spend more than a fraction of their new revenues. The world currencies system, though showing more immediate resilience to sudden shock under the regime of floating exchange rates than it formerly showed, is really no system at all; and it is certainly no longer anchored to any objective standard, or value, or discipline, which can counteract against whatever inflationary tendencies there may be in the collective actions of the world's leading governments, most of whom depend on democratic consent.

But Matter considered that even before the outbreak of the energy crises, inflation in most western industrial nations has been climbing at such a rate that it threatens to become self-generating, as more and more people seek to anticipate rising prices by buying in advance. To some extent, a flight into real assets was already in progress and there were signs that the capital markets were feeling the backlash. The quadrupling of the price of oil and the boom on the other commodity markets had undeniably helped to stoke inflation. But the entire blame cannot be placed on the door of the raw material exporters. To some extent, their demands were a reaction to the inflation in the industrial nations.

In the seven largest member countries of the OECD – Canada, the United States, Japan, France, Germany, Italy and the United Kingdom – the cost of living went up by an average rate of 14.8% in the first six months of 1974. Japan was at the top of the league with 29.8% and Germany at the bottom with 7.8%. It is a familiar fact that the steeper the rate of inflation, the more painful is the adjustment process necessary for normalisation. Economic overheating and inflation-inspired flights into real assets lead to mis-investments, which have to be rectified.

The first six months of 1974 saw not only a surge in inflation in the majority of Western industrial nations, but a simultaneous slowdown in growth, bordering in some cases on recession. The slackening trend had already been visible in the latter half of 1973, when capacity had reached full strength in many sectors. In addition, several industrial countries, faced with steady currency erosions, were compelled to adopt restrictive monetary measures which caused a shortage of liquidity and a gradual dampening of demand.

The oil crises gave the down-swing added impetus. It had been estimated that in 1974 the oil-exporters stood to receive about $60 billion of extra revenue, most of which had to be raised by the industrial nations of Western Europe. A transfer of wealth on such a scale as this is not something which can be accomplished overnight. The oil-importing countries are going to have to divert part of their production away from their domestic markets and into exports: this requires a radical restructuring, a process which could take years and be accompanied, temporarily, by recessive tendencies. The capacity of the Middle East states, however, to absorb supplementary supplies of goods and services was at present very limited, and they can only spend a fraction of their new-found wealth on their new-found imports. On the basis of revised estimates released by the OECD and the IMF, the additional foreign exchange bill resulting from the oil crisis, which cannot be met by boosting exports to the Arab countries, is likely to amount to $40 billion in 1974 for the industrial nations, and to $10 billion for those developing countries which have no oil of their own. The situation will only change in the process of time, as Arab economic development steadily progresses. The part of the oil revenues which they choose to save instead of spending will inevitably leave a gap in income. It does not need to be accompanied by a drop in demand, since the country affected could save less or, alternatively, borrow more. In view of the sheer magnitude of the funds accumulating in Arab hands, it is hardly conceivable that this short-fall in income can be fully compensated.

Jay was equally gloomy about the oil situation. Neither conservation and oil economy measures nor development of alternative energy resources in the consuming nations will drastically reduce demand for oil by the end of the decade, though big changes might be made during 1980.

He assumed oil prices would move in such a way to ensure a wide, though not necessarily widening, imbalance of payments and current accounts for the oil-producing and oil-consuming countries lasting into the 1980s; but Britain will likely be getting substantial imports of oil by the end of this decade; but by that time it will have quite heavily mortgaged future oil reserves to serve the huge investment in exploration and extraction of North Sea oil and to service and repay international borrowing and help, in financing six years of heavy balance of payments deficits; the oil-producing countries will continue to be ready to supply substantially the amount of oil required by the oil-consuming countries, though at a price which will continue to be much higher than anything to which we were accustomed in 1973 – problems, in other words, will continue until the end of the 1970s.

Jay considered that the consuming countries' oil deficits will be financed, in part, by a growing volume of expenditure in investment by some of the oil-producing countries. The rest, he feared, will be financed by the rapid creation of new international money, which was what had happened during the first seven months of 1974 when virtually the whole of the oil-producing countries' gain in reserves was provided out of newly created world reserve assets. World inflationary trends will be progressively accelerated, fuelled and lubricated by this situation, towards a general financial breakdown. The implication for the oil-producing countries is that they will get paid good prices for oil, but that they will be paid in highly vulnerable, indeed, in progressively self-extinguishing, assets. Assuming that the option of withholding the oil is not open, for over-riding, geo-political reasons, or for reasons of economic development, then it will be important to convert cash as quickly as possible into sound long-term investments.

The more that those can be made within the territorial frontiers and jurisdiction of the oil-producing countries, the safer will they be from expropriation by the increasingly desperate oil-consuming countries.

Economic Tightrope

Massive payments deficits are hanging like a sword of Damocles over a number of countries, said Matter.

Only a few of them, West Germany and Switzerland for

instance, are fortunate enough to be able to finance their deficits with surpluses on their balance of payments items. But the great majority have no option but to deflate demand and finance the short-fall through international borrowings. Any all-round tightening of the belt has to be ruled out, as the cumulative effect will be to plunge the world economy into wholesale recession. It is unanimously agreed that they all have to come to terms with these deficits. In view of the massive sums involved, drawing on monetary reserves will at best only provide a temporary respite and, even if official gold reserves are to be remobilised at a market-related price, the effect, on balance, will hardly be more than a drop in the ocean. Italy – one of the handful of countries with substantial stocks of monetary gold – had to fall back on this last-ditch reserve at the end of August 1974, in order to stave off international insolvency and national bankruptcy. In return for a $2 billion loan from West Germany, the Banca d'Italia pledged 515 tons of gold as collateral.

The funds needed to finance the deficits will, in point of fact, be available, since the bulk of the Arab oil money will in all likelihood be reinvested somewhere abroad. The snag is that those countries which are most heavily in debt are also those which experience the most difficulty in obtaining credit.

Breaking this vicious circle will be the crux of the re-cycling problem. Although the process of adjustment to the quad-rupling of the price of oil has barely begun, serious difficulties are already being encountered.

A growing number of remedies have been proposed. They range from re-cycling, an up-dated version of the Marshal plan, to radical cures like guerrilla warfare and military intervention. No concrete progress was made at the IMF annual meeting towards extracting countries from the oil disaster. The Fund's executive directors have been given the task of producing specific proposals for amplifying the oil facilities, with a view to channeling more of the surplus oil revenues to the needy importing countries. But at present these efforts seem unlikely to meet with great success since, as time goes by, it has become increasingly obvious that only a limited amount of funds can be mobilised for re-cycling purposes, no matter what form this re-cycling takes. It had already become clear in the summer of 1974 that financial markets and banks were not able to offer the producing countries adequate guarantees as prime debtors, nor to assume the creditor risk in respect of countries which were heavily in debt and struggling with large payments deficits. Apart from this, they are incapable of converting the oil money, which is predominately invested as short-term, into long-term loans necessary to finance the deficits, without themselves running into liquidity difficulties. A gradual reduction in money-market rates, which is now in progress in various countries, might have encouraged the oil producers to look around for longer term investments and thus help to restore a better concordance of maturities.

Scope for redistributing the petrodollars through the IMF and other international organisations is also limited.

The British scheme, to create a special agency within the IMF, the German plan to set up an international bank, as well as projects to increase the financial resources of the world bank, all ultimately depend on whether the OPEC countries are prepared to supply the necessary funds. So far they have only been willing to do so if they could count on an attractive return and if they, themselves, had to bear virtually no risk. (In January 1975 the nine EEC countries agreed to the British scheme put forward by Chancellor Denis Healey to establish a system of re-cycling £5,000 million of Arab Oil Money through IMF. The money will be borrowed by IMF and then re-lent to members in balance of payments difficulties for periods of three to seven years. The EEC countries were not in favour of an American proposal put forward by U.S. Secretary of State Dr Henry Kissinger, that OECD countries should re-lend each other funds flowing from the oil producers.) Apart from the oil producers the only remaining potential guarantors are the United States and a handful of industrial countries whose balance of payments are still in surplus.

The United States has made it abundantly clear on more than

one occasion that, in her role as the re-cycler of petrodollars, she is not prepared to act as liberal guarantor for all those countries which are so heavily in debt that the risk for private banks has already become too great and which, for the same reason, are receiving only limited assistance from the oil producers.

The United States and the remaining hard-currency countries would have to bear a disproportionately high liability, not only in the case of direct aid, but also in respect of financial arrangements through the IMF and the World Bank, since very few of the oil-exporting countries are represented in these organisations. Unless the producing countries, therefore, are prepared to assume at least some part of the risk, no large-scale re-cycling schemes are likely to materialise.

The question of liability has also been at the centre of discussions dealing with the terms and conditions of an EEC loan to be launched by member countries in order to bridge over oil deficits. It has been agreed that if a country finds itself unable to repay its borrowings, those member states whose payments are in balance or surplus must intervene on its behalf. The maximum cover obligation of the three member countries – Germany, France and the United Kingdom – does not however exceed 44% of the total value of the loan. This means that, if the worst comes to the worst, potential creditors in the oil countries would have to seek repayment of the outstanding portion of the debt from a country which is insolvent. It still remains to be seen what the reaction will be to such a scheme. The $3 billion saving set for the loan in 1975 seems rather modest alongside the oil deficit of $15 billion estimated for the European Economic Community as a whole.

There has been a growing realisation that the necessary funds available will only come in trickles, not only at present but probably in the future, and that the effect of re-cycling will merely be to postpone, not solve, the problems. In the long run, payments deficits will not be patched up by borrowing.

Several countries are already saddled with such huge debts that there is little prospect of their ever being able to repay them. The American attitude is that the present level of the oil price is unacceptable and, if world-wide recession and disintegration are to be averted, an alliance of oil-consuming countries in the so-called "group of twelve" is likely to be viewed with growing interest.

It is intended that this group, which consists of the United States, Canada, Japan and Norway, the Common Market members with the exception of France, would not only take action in the event of oil supplies being cut back, or boycott measures being imposed, but also contribute towards closer co-operation in the field of energy-policy. However, as far as this latter objective is concerned, the programme remains vague. It seems unlikely that the American aim, of forcing OPEC on to the defensive by cutting back oil consumption and preventing the inflow of petrodollars into those countries with payment surpluses, can be achieved in this way. Above all, it seems doubtful whether a will to make any real energy savings exists.

The prime considerations guiding Arab investment policy are security and liquidity. As shrewd financiers, they not only look for yields, but also protection from inflation and transfer restrictions. They are not interested in amassing currencies in which their assets would be steadily eaten away by inflation and depreciation. They are seeking some form of guarantee that, with the money now flowing to them, they will at least be able to purchase at a future date approximately the same quality of goods as they can at the present time.

Countries, like Italy,[1] which are heavily in debt, threatened by insolvency and plagued by exceptionally virulent inflation, can therefore hardly expect oil money to be spontaneously channelled their way on any scale. In view of the rate of inflation even in countries with relatively stable economies, the Arabs have already envisaged possibilities like indexing the price of oil. Plans to create a single Arab currency for inter-

---

1 At the beginning of 1975, U.S. President Gerald Ford in an interview with the well-known commentator William Alsop indicated that he expected one Western European country to go bankrupt in 1975. Though he did not name the country it was generally agreed that he was referring to Italy.

national transactions, as well as an Arab capital market to safeguard against monetary losses, appear to be at this moment castles in the air. Years must elapse before such projects can be realised, if indeed they are feasible at all. But Arab demands for investments with a stable money-value and secure exchange rate cannot be taken lightly, for in a medium or longer-range perspective – more so than at short-term where there would be certain technical obstacles – they are in a position to cut back their production if they find no secure outlets for investing their income.

The present trend among oil producers is to invest predominantly at very short-term and, in doing so, to keep all their options open. Initially, a substantial amount of petrodollars reached the Eurocurrency market, where they earned high rates of interest. Acting on the principle, "first come, first served", those countries which were hardest hit by oil deficits began to scramble for Euroloans. According to figures published in the IMF Survey, Euroloans totalling nearly $20 billion were granted in the first six months of 1974, compared with $20 billion for the whole of 1973. Two-thirds of this total went to the industrial nations. Britain secured the lion's share with $4.8 billion, followed by France with $2.9 billion and Italy with $2.2 billion, whereas the Arabs invested their capital only at extremely short-term. What is needed to remedy payments *disequilibria* are long-dated funds with a maturity of several years. The Eurobond market would have been a suitable instrument; however, worldwide inflation, soaring short-term interest rates and the exchange rate uncertainty had seriously impaired its ability to function.

The net result has been that short-term investments on the Eurocurrency market had to be redeployed on an increasing scale at medium or long-term in the form of "roll-over" loans. When the risks of the Euromarket began to become all too apparent around the middle of 1974, the hectic level of activity was followed by a lull. The discrepancy between maturities, coupled with the increased risk attached to floating rates, led to alarming losses and bank failures. The fact that the Euromarket operates in some degree of secrecy and is not subject to supervision proved to be a distinct drawback. Only the really first-class Eurobanks can hope to raise money on the Euro-market. Countries heavily in debt like Italy and Britain, and developing nations with no raw materials of their own, are coming up against mistrust.

For reasons of security, more and more investors have stayed away from the Euromarket, turning instead to the traditional money-markets in London and New York. New York hit the jackpot, but London also derived considerable benefit, at least for a time. Oil deliveries from Iran, Kuwait, Abu Dhabi, Qatar, Nigeria and, to some extent, from Saudi Arabia were paid for in sterling. The international oil companies maintained short-term sterling positions in London; so far, these positions have never been fully converted by the Middle East recipients. The attraction of New York as a money-market lies in its enormous capacity, backed by the mighty U.S. economy, which is still by far the most potent in the world. Since the resignation of ex-President Nixon in August 1974, the political uncertainty which had been weighing heavily on the economy was dispelled and the dollar strengthened and the flow of oil money, which had already been considerable, gathered new impetus. Some oil producers even began to change their pounds for dollars. Customers from the Middle East are currently buying up large amounts of marketable and non-marketable American Treasury Bills. The main buyers are reported to be Saudi Arabia and Kuwait.

So far, the oil-producing nations, where they *have* invested, have concentrated on the property market, mainly in the United States, but also in Britain. Iran's holding in Krupp, one of the most traditional of Germany's industrial groups, has been an isolated case so far.[2]

As their surplus revenues continue to accumulate, there is a strong likelihood that the oil producers will be obliged to look around for medium and long-term investment outlets. Whether

2 In February 1975, Iran invested £100 million in Pan American Airways.

or not Europe will receive its share will depend in large measure on how successful most countries are in regaining control of their errant economies. The investment of petrodollars at longer term would be doubly welcome. Firstly, the threat of monetary crisis would be sensibly diminished if the amount of volatile and highly liquid capital around was reduced. Secondly, by forging closer ties with Western industrial nations, the oil producers themselves have a vested interest in not provoking any crisis. If they decided to resort to tactics like cutting back oil deliveries, they would to some extent be harming their own interest.

It soon became apparent that the Euromarket would be unable, in the long run, to fulfill the great hopes pinned on it in respect of re-cycling funds to those countries hardest hit by dearer oil prices but least able to help themselves. The search has begun for other sources of finance to supplement the private markets. In the meantime several funds have been set up, but with all too few resources. A group of oil-producing countries have placed funds to the value of $2.8 billion Special Drawing Rights at the disposal of the IMF. The so-called "oil facility" will be made available to needy countries to help them cover their oil deficits. In addition, the Arab Investment Company has been recently founded with a capital of $200 million. Other resources are to be allocated through the World Bank. All these amounts are relatively small and probably total no more than $5 to $6 billion altogether. They are modest beginnings but fall far short of what is needed. If the problem of re-cycling is to be solved and a worldwide recession averted, even more intensive efforts will be required at international level.

The elimination of the energy crisis is still a very distant prospect surrounded by many imponderables. What is certain is that a large measure of goodwill and a readiness to concede and co-operate will be necessary if the crisis is to be overcome without serious and irreparable consequences for the consumer and producer countries alike. In the industrialised nations it will be particularly painful for social groups accustomed to years of uninterrupted growth and steadily rising prosperity to face the unpalatable realisation that times have definitely changed.

Steep inflation, marginal or even negative growth, payments deficits and unsound financing practices all add up to a highly explosive mixture which makes economic policy in many countries an extremely delicate operation. The fact that the more-or-less restrictive money policies adopted in most countries have tended to dampen demand rather than check rising prices, can certainly be attributed to dearer oil and the general shortage of raw material, but also, to no small extent, to constantly rising wages and salaries. The great increase in the oil price is a one-time occurrence. The situation on the commodity markets has eased somewhat in the meantime. However, there seems little prospect of oil becoming cheaper, since the producing countries have already demonstrated that they prefer to cut back supplies rather than lower prices.

A problem which cannot be taken seriously enough, however, is the pressure on costs caused by excessive wage increases which, in a climate of monetary restrictions, exert a recessionary influence, especially since in most countries wages are tied in varying degrees to the cost of living index.

The belief that "cost-push" inflation and the vicious circle of the wage-price spiral can be mastered by a prices and incomes policy has proved, time and again, to be an illusion, because the price controls cannot be put into practice, because the wage pattern is disrupted by strike action, or because wages and prices are shot up to double the rate once the controls are lifted and quickly neutralise any successes achieved.

At present, a number of countries are seeking to escape the clutches of "stagflation" by resorting to a two-pronged strategy. Higher public expenditure and tax incentives are being used to secure employment, whilst money policy is being geared to curbing prices and improving the balance of payments. However, there is a limit to the extent to which money and financial policy can run in contradictory directions. If money policy is so restrictive that the State, with one hand, takes away in the form of credit controls the benefits it has given the private sector with the other, there can be no overall increase of demand. The policy might even tend to accentuate the downtrend, since the effect of financing public deficits through the money and capital markets is to boost rising interest rates still further, thus causing a damper on the stock markets, already depressed, and causing the climate for shares and bonds to deteriorate.

In the latter half of 1974 the expected improvement in the economic situation of most countries did not take place to the hoped for extent. The result was a drastic revision downwards: credit restrictions, if not abandoned, were made more lenient. But relaxing credit restrictions, or even relinquishing them, has no less a disastrous effect than if they are applied too restrictively. The impact on growth would be relatively marginal and lead to a new surge in prices and wages and a deterioration in the payments situation. The course which economic policy must steer between the Scylla of inflation and the Charybadis of unemployment and recession is a very narrow one.

Success, according to Matter, depends fundamentally on two factors:

1. the wage trend and the attitude of the unions;
2. the ability to gauge correctly the external influences.

Unions are aware that no government can afford unemployment on any sizeable scale and that people in the majority of Western industrial nations, accustomed to many years of prosperity, will not accept that lean years must follow, with unemployment, when the growth of real income is virtually static.

They are secure in the knowledge that governments have no alternative but to give timely boosts in order to avert political and industrial unrest. The unions have, so far, shown little sign of moderating their demands, despite the looming threat of crisis, and if the attitude persists and the unions emerge victors in the game of industrial poker, the result will be a wave of inflation which will sooner or later culminate in catastrophe. It is vital, therefore, that the unions back the governments in their efforts to master a difficult situation, instead of attacking them from the rear.

Future Prospects

Jay was much more pessimistic about the future than Matter. The broad prospect he held out was a continuation, and even an intensification, of the cyclical "boom and bust" pattern of the last decade, with a progressive acceleration from cycle to cycle in the going rate of inflation. This will eventually lead to a "bust" of an altogether different order from the cyclical down-swings between the four yearly booms of the past. The progressive assault on monetary values and currency stability will wreak its revenge – unless one can believe in the possibility of an effective world-wide incomes policy in the industrialised nations. When money no longer performs its economic function, a severe world depression must be expected to follow. How long it might last would depend on how long it took to establish an effective and accepted world-wide currency reform and to generate general confidence that the new money would not rapidly go the way of the old money.

The recession which has taken place has provided, to a limited extent, an antidote to inflation. There has been a fall in some commodity prices, and it is likely to continue, perhaps with increasing momentum, as economic activity in the industrialised countries continues to weaken. The fall in commodity prices, oil excluded, can affect the going rate of inflation in the main industrial countries and ease it during 1975. But a very strong "ratchet effect" is built into the response of inflation to the booms and slumps in world trade. Commodity prices which are fairly freely set in world markets might respond quite swiftly downwards as well as upwards. A much more important constituent, however, labour costs, does not show any such symmetrical flexibility. Not only do labour costs almost never fall, but their rate of increase is often quite insensitive to the state of demand in the labour market.

This was probably less true outside Western Europe than within it. When governments react, as they had in the autumn of 1973, to the inflationary pressures building up in their economies by limiting the growth of their domestic money supplies, an effect greatly magnified by the impact of the oil-induced payments which developed from the beginning of 1974, they begin to move into recession. When all countries are doing the same thing, there is no escape from this by increasing exports, except at the risk of beggaring one's neighbours and one's neighbours beggaring one. If the process continues long enough, there will be a point when the degree of recession in the industrial countries will just match the forces in the labour markets which prevent pay from adjusting downwards in conditions of declining demand. Inflation – domestically generated cost inflation – will then stop, but at a very high continuing level of unemployment. Long before that stage democratic governments will reverse the levers of monetary and fiscal policy in order to restore full employment at whatever risks to renewed inflation. The process has begun in the United States, Britain, and in Western Europe.

Whatever cyclical relief might happen to the inflation which grips the world, therefore, will only be temporary. Only if the governments of the major industrial countries, which are also for the most part the great democracies, are willing to countenance years of mass unemployment, without taking any fiscal or monetary counter-action, will it be plausible to expect any secular or long-term abatement of inflation. It is rather more probable that strong reflationary action in the major economies, before the end of 1975, will have the world economy expanding at full blast – in fact straining to exceed the limits of "full blast" by 1977. At the top of the boom inflation will again have surged ahead, starting from a higher base level, and will surpass the peaks reached in the summer of 1974. The "ratchet" would then operate to ensure that any relief thereafter could only be temporary, cyclical and partial.

The prospects for the U.K. appeared to Jay to be a particularly vivid microcosm of the world prospects. A recession during the current year, with some short-term alleviation of price pressures because of steadier import prices, would trigger reflationary measures whose vigour would grow as the recession deepens. Almost cynically, he saw the most vigorous measures being taken – as in the winter of 1972–73 and before – after the nadir of the recession had already passed, with the equally usual consequence that the recovery would be too rapid and overdone, thereby precipitating an abrupt deterioration in the trade balance and an early reappearance of shortages and renewed inflationary pressures.

Timing was, he admitted, a most difficult thing to predict with any confidence. But, as with the world economy, a rough guide would make 1975 the year of recession accompanied by reflationary measures, 1976 the year of sluggish recovery and further reflationary measures, and 1977 the year of sharp upturn and then crisis. This will be superimposed on a situation of quite abnormal inflationary and balance of payments experience in the recession years. Because of the oil deficit and lost competitiveness in 1973 and 1974, the balance of payments seems likely to remain in substantial deficit even in the recession years, something which did not happen in 1952, 1958, 1962, 1966, or 1971. A sharp deterioration in 1977, super-added to existing substantial deficits in 1975 and 1976, and super-added to a situation in which Britain will have already accumulated unprecedented foreign debts, many of them in an unstable form of short-term deposits in sterling by oil-producing states, is not a happy one.

"This next cycle will be lucky if inflation gets as low as 10% at its minimum point, that is if Denis Healey's pre-election prediction for the end of 1975 were fulfilled on his highly sanguine assumption that the social contract is carried out to the letter – if an unwritten contract can be fulfilled to the letter – between now and then," said Jay. "Super-add to this the normal process of pay-push inflation *and* the near inevitability of some further substantial depreciation of sterling over the next few years *and* renewed overheating of the home market in 1977 *and* a probable world commodity price boom in that year, then there is the prospect of inflation in 1977 running at an extraordinary rate," was his gloomy forecast.

Matter felt that unnecessary pessimism served only to damage as it inevitably prejudiced decisions focused on the future. Also, too much despondency tended to obscure the clarity of judgment which is more essential at the present time than ever before in economic policy.

He agreed with Jay that inflation rates might tend to ease in the near future, but that a too-vigorous breakout from economic recession will lend renewed impetus to rising prices. It is of paramount importance that potential external influences were gauged correctly and that the kind of protectionist measures which brought about the collapse of world trade in the thirties be avoided. During 1975 there would be a lean period which might extend into 1976 and it would be a long time before the growth rates of the fifties and sixties were experienced again.

The economic outlook in Europe is a sombre one, especially with a recession taking place in the United States, where the economy during 1974 was in a state of negative growth; calculated on the annual basis, the real Gross National Product during the first nine months dropped by 7% in the first quarter, by 1.6% in the second, and by 2.9% in the third. The downtrend took place particularly in housing and the automobile industry. Capital expenditure, although quantitatively high, is on the decline, and private consumption is static at constant prices. The excessive speculative demand for commodities is likely to fade this year and there could be some pressure to run down excess stocks, even if it causes losses in the process. The Federal Reserve Bank reported that industrial firms were operating at only 79.2% of maximum capacity in the third quarter of 1974, compared with 80.1% in the second quarter, and 83.3% twelve months previously. In September 1974 the jobless rate was running at 5.8% and the August 1974 trade balance was the biggest monthly shortfall in American history at $1.13 billion. Consumer prices were up 12.1% compared to the previous year, and were tending to rise.

The developments in the United States will undoubtedly affect Europe and the European Economic Commission estimated that the real growth of GNP for the Common Market as a whole was 2.5% for 1974, compared with 5.6% in 1973. Only France, Italy and the Benelux countries will exceed this average. Real demand for consumer and capital goods is flagging. The Commission estimated that the combined current account deficit of all its members *vis-à-vis* third countries would total £20 billion in 1974, compared with a surplus of £1 billion in 1973. The Commission had hopes that the imbalances would be reduced this year and that growth conditions would gradually improve so that the increase in real GNP will be in the order of 3.5% – but it is unlikely to be achieved with the surveys and forecasts made in various countries indicating a continued downward trend.

"In spite of the uncertain and not altogether rosy outlook, there is no justification for evoking the spectre of the thirties," said Matter. "On the evidence available so far, we cannot speak of a general process of contraction in the world economy."

chapter 2

Scotland's Prospects

The problem of development in an economy substantially exposed to international trade and investment is essentially the problem of achieving a market-clearing price for labour, asserted Peter Jay.

And he thought that it was at least illuminating to see Scotland as a unitary economy which happened, for historical reasons, to form part of the United Kingdom currency area. It threw light not only on the problem of Scottish development, which was regarded as a problem of regional development, but also by analogy on the problem of British development, if and when the U.K. economy became part of a wider common-market currency area.

The suggestion that market forces are a consideration in economic thought, or that keeping labour costs down might be one of the better ways of achieving desired prosperity, has numerous and extremely vocal critics. He was not, however, dismissing natural resources and geographical advantages as unimportant in determining the wealth of nations, and in explaining the differences in the wealth of nations. But they are unchanging factors – even an asset like North Sea oil will only give the lucky possessor a once-and-for-all benefit, in the sense of a permanent improvement in living standards, provided the opportunities are prudently exploited.

"But such factors are unlikely to be discovered again and

37

again as part of the normal routine of any economy, and they certainly lie outside the power of governments and economic planners to create."

The governments and economic planners can, however, influence, or refrain from inhibiting, the rate at which an economy takes advantage of its natural endowments of geography, resources, population and know-how.

The absorptive capacity of world markets was almost infinite in relation to an economy of the size of Scotland or Britain. So, too, is the supply of capital and know-how throughout the world. It is a matter of looking for the right place to locate the economic activities which supply the world's market. (Obviously technical, specialist manpower and market proximity requirements with certain products limited the choice.)

The determining factor, therefore, about where investment goes and why some economies and regions suffer unemployment and others surge ahead, is *cost* and *profitability*. The world's savings tend, at the margin, to be attracted to the areas of best return. Wherever that turns out to be, jobs are plentiful and wages high and rising. The opposite takes place in areas of poor return to investment.

There is, unfortunately, a fundamental distinction between *crude* labour-cost comparisons (labour-cost per unit of output between two areas of the same economies) and *adjusted* labour-cost comparisons (labour-cost per unit of output, net of all other differences in cost per unit of output including transport, marketing and other costs entering into the final price). The cheapest place to produce is where the adjusted labour costs are lowest, although that will not necessarily be where crude labour costs are lowest, still less where wages are lowest.

Jay believed – accepting substantial exposure to world trade and investment, and a geographical and cultural environment basically hospitable to industrial activity – that the key to rapid development is adjusted labour-cost. If they are above the levels in alternative economies and regions, investment will shy away, jobs will be lost, wages will fall behind and the whole cycle of economic depression takes place. Conversely, internationally-competitive, adjusted labour-costs – an economy or region enjoying a world market clearing price for labour, leaving all other factors as they happen to be – will produce rapid growth and a dynamic prosperity.

The argument might be put forward that such a theory cannot apply, since Maynard Keynes showed how to maintain full employment and the fact that governments are active in the extended public sector as investors and employers. But Jay considered that his thesis applied equally well to all national economies or whole currency areas as to regions within economies and to economies within currency areas. It is the realisation of an important truth that lay behind the doctrines of the new Cambridge school, that the level of economic activity in an economy should be regulated by exchange rate adjustments and that substantial economic growth could only take place through export growth.

A currency area as a whole, which thought to spend its way out of unemployment when its *adjusted* labour-costs were above world levels, would find its balance of payments plunging into deficit before full employment was restored.

"That essentially was the story of British economic policy over the decade or so before the 1967 devaluation. It could well be the position again now, although the effects of the oil-producing countries' surpluses following the 1974 winter increase in oil prices make the facts more than usually difficult to interpret."

The way to restore domestic and external equilibrium in such a situation is to adjust the exchange rate for the currency in a way as to bring adjusted labour-costs into line with world standards – to restore the competitiveness of the nation's or area's industry. It would happen automatically in free currency markets, and only the grossest of all interference in price-mechanism's fixed exchange-rates would obstruct the process of adjustment and make possible the prolonged periods of uncompetitiveness and economic stagnation which Britain suffered in the post-war period.

The position of Scotland, as an economy within a wider

39

common currency area, was that an exchange-rate adjustment with the outside world (a major part of which, in terms of investment and trade, was the rest of the United Kingdom) was ruled out by the very fact of having a common currency.

"I have always felt," said Jay, "that were I an economic adviser to the Scottish National Party it is this fact beyond all others that I would urge as the primary object of complaint and as the first priority of change.

"For, once let adjusted labour-costs in Scotland move out of line with those in the rest of the U.K., especially if those in the rest of the U.K. tend to be out of line with those in the rest of the industrial world, and the Scottish economy becomes doomed to a progressive debility. Nor is it likely that such debility can ever be more than marginally mitigated by even the most energetic efforts of the London government to steer investment towards Scotland by subsidising capital costs."

Professor D. I. MacKay of Aberdeen University, in a paper entitled "North Sea Oil and the Scottish Economy", presented before the 1974 British Association for the Advancement of Science at Stirling, had said:

"A regional policy, although it has certainly been of considerable assistance to the developing areas, has never been able to provide the major structural shift which is necessary to achieve more rapid economic growth. It is this shift which is essential for a fundamental change in the prospects of development areas such as Scotland. Regional policy should not begin and end with a question of manipulating effective demand, which is much less important than many regional economists suppose.

"In essence what is required is a change in the pattern of production . . ."

Jay was not sure that Professor MacKay's concept of changing the pattern of production was quite the same as his own of ensuring the external competitiveness of Scottish industry, by keeping *adjusted* labour-costs at, or a little below, world levels and leaving most of the rest to market forces. But he agreed with Professor MacKay when he said:

"We are talking about what Sir John Hicks in the context of the theory of fluctuations and Professor Tom Wilson in the context of regional development called the 'super multiplier'; something more complex, more dynamic and certainly more unpredictable than the simple and mechanistic Keynsian multiplier." Jay also agreed with MacKay's acid judgment:

"An investigation of how we arrived at a policy which envisages capital-intensive development in areas of labour shortage would make an interesting thesis, but it certainly owes nothing to first principles!"

But why should *adjusted* labour-costs in Scotland move out of line with those outside in the first place? There were many reasons, according to Jay – including the reasons commonly cited for Scotland's economic decline after the hey-day of those particular heavy and extractive industries on which Scotland's original prosperity was based.

When industries for which Scotland had particular advantages, like shipbuilding and coal-mining, entered a secular decline, for whatever reasons, jobs had to be found, if at all, in other industries. If these had equal non-labour-cost advantages with the traditional industries they would have been traditional industries themselves. It was therefore likely that, if *adjusted* labour-costs were not to be higher in the new industries than in the old, then *crude* labour-costs would have to be lower.

Since productivity tended to be given and wages were sticking downwards, the adjustment was most unlikely to occur, at least to the extent necessary. Because the exchange-rate adjustment was impossible within a single currency area, therefore, the regional economy found the initial, once-and-for-all penalty of losing traditional industries, which had comparative international advantages, transformed into a perpetual dynamic of decay.

It could be argued that the fault then lay with the process of collective bargaining which prevented wages from adjusting to the new circumstances and so kept adjusted labour-costs above internationally-competitive levels. Formerly, this way of putting the point was not false. But, from the point of view of the policy-maker, it is more useful to focus attention on the things which he could change, rather than on the things which he could not change.

The question then arises whether the policy-maker can operate directly on adjusted labour-costs when a determination of money wages is beyond his control. He certainly can operate on adjusted labour-costs measured in terms of international currency, if he can exchange the exchange-rate for a domestic currency (provided, of course, that domestic wages do not then rise to the previous international value). But that is ruled out for the policy-maker in a regional economy.

He can, alternatively, operate on adjusted labour-cost by trying to bring down non-labour-costs. But for reasons which Professor MacKay indicated, such a method of trying to establish a market clearing price for labour owed more to Humpty Dumpty's logic than to first principles of political economy.

What then remains? The answer appears to be direct subsidy of labour-cost. It is not an original thought. But there has been the Selective Employment Premium, the Regional Employment Premium, and the suggestion put forward by the National Economic Development Office for a percentage *regional payroll subsidy*.

There is a wide-spread aversion to subsidies, especially in the minds of those who attach importance to market forces. But Jay made the point that the payroll subsidies are entirely consistent with the free market philosophy. The purpose is purely and exclusively to achieve that adjustment in adjusted labour-costs which would be brought about by market forces not distorted by the downward stickiness of wages and the artificiality of a fixed, indeed immutable, exchange-rate between two parts of a single currency area. That is a man-made rigidity and it justifies compensating, man-made adjustments, designed to restore the balance of supply and demand on the basis of that market clearing price for labour which market forces would bring about if they are not inhibited. But where was the revenue to come from to pay the tax? The important thing is that it would be an economically-mutual tax. Income tax was a candidate, but was unsatisfactory in the sense that higher income taxes might persuade employees to press for extra increases in pay to restore their post-tax disposable incomes in money terms. If they were successful, it would frustrate the purpose of the payroll subsidy. Therefore general indirect taxation, in Britain's case at present the Value Added Tax, is a better alternative. The effect on prices of the payroll subsidy for goods produced for the home market would just offset the effects of the extra Value Added Tax. Imports would suffer the effects of the increased VAT, while exports would enjoy the full benefit of a payroll subsidy. If the revenue was not Scottish revenue but British revenue, then the regional economy would enjoy, in addition, a transfer of resources from outside, equivalent to the value of the subsidy (less that part of it which was attributable to taxes collected in Scotland).

But Jay did not consider that regional development has become an anachronism with North Sea oil and the investment in what is regarded as Scotland's new prosperous future. He considered that to think in that way was to show an optimism which ran beyond what he regarded were the facts. Again he quoted from MacKay's paper in support of this view:

"The cases I have put forward would suggest that North Sea oil activities might lead directly to the creation of some 25,000/30,000 additional jobs. This employment will be highly concentrated and will transform the economic prospects of certain areas . . . However, these lie outside the industrial heartland of the country, and in particular are removed from the Clydeside area which is the focus of the greatest social and economic problems. It is therefore quite possible that the direct impact from North Sea oil will still leave Clydeside, and hence the Scottish economy as a whole, with the familiar problems of low incomes, high unemployment and high emigration . . . My own view would be that the direct impact of North Sea oil and gas offers too narrow and restricted an industrial base to transform the prospects for the whole of the Scottish economy.

"The magnitude of this task is formidable. The estimate of primary North Sea job creation for 25,000/30,000 has its limitations, but even if we bear these in mind, we have to set the estimates against a known rate of job loss in the primary, manufacturing and extractive sectors of Scotland which amounted to no less than 26,000 jobs per annum over 1966/72, a period in which Scotland did relatively well compared to economic performance in the 1950s and early 1960s. Hence while the direct impact of North Sea oil will be important in providing a new and significant growth sector, something more will be needed."

Jay's own conclusion was that, to ensure a prosperous future for Scotland with the highest sustainable wage level, the fullest practicable employment and the lowest feasible rate of economically-enforced emigration, *the priority for action at government level – whether in London or in Edinburgh – will have to be ensuring a market clearing price for labour, perhaps using the technique of a general payroll subsidy,* if an independent Scottish currency with its own external exchange-rate was not deemed worth the inconvenience of forfeiting the advantages of a single currency area throughout the United Kingdom. If that condition is ensured, then investment will follow. He had no doubts that the entrepreneurial talents of the Scottish people, the quality of its work force, the good fortune of its geography, and the excellent service of its bankers, made Scotland an ideal host to rapid industrial progress – granted only the dynamic precondition which he had outlined.

In contrast, Alfred Matter thought that the oil bonanza would ensure Scotland a bright future, despite the problems which have to be overcome.

The economic outlook for Britain in 1975 is not altogether rosy. The country is in the grip of an acute bout of stagflation. Oil deficits are pushing the trade balance deep into the red, and inflows of foreign capital, sometimes on a considerable scale – partly from the oil nations – have kept the pressure off the monetary reserves and buoyed up the pound. Any sudden, extensive withdrawal of these funds can, however, quickly bring sterling to the brink of crisis.

North Sea oil promised rescue from this rather gloomy situation. With the energy crisis and the soaring price of oil it has become more competitive. The cost of extracting it is many times higher than for the Arab states as the fuels are off-shore ones, posing immense technical problems. But by 1980 Britain hopes to be a net exporter of North Sea oil. The revenues which accrue will be used in part to repay the loans which are currently necessary to finance deficits of current accounts.

For Scotland, there are prospects of large-scale investment in drilling rigs and auxiliary plant as well as inflows of foreign capital in the years ahead. Exploiting the oilfield will make investments necessary in many other areas – the infrastructure would have to be developed; housing requirements and consumption would increase, in line with the growing number employed and rising incomes.

A Payroll Subsidy – But How?

How would a payroll subsidy help Scotland? How different is it to the Regional Employment Premium? Would it not lead to feather-bedding industries which are uneconomic? Two peers, Lord Balfour of Burleigh, a director of the Bank of Scotland, and Lord Taylor of Gryfe, Chairman of British Rail in Scotland, and trades unionist Andrew Forman, Divisional Officer of the Union of Shop, Distributive and Allied Workers, were to the fore in raising such questions.

And are the British public, management and trades unions aware of the problem of inflation? To what extent would the Social Contract, devised by the Labour Government and the TUC, help excessive wage demands in the future?

Forman raised the question of "feather-bedding". Was the payroll subsidy to be a permanent feature?

"I have no objection as such, but I think some of us (trades unionists) get worried a little by this subsidising of a pay bill, if it has the effect of feather-bedding employers, who then have very little of an incentive to improve their performance, both management-wise and in production."

It was Forman too who raised the problem of the Social Contract. Almost defensively at first, over Matter's reference to the unions showing little signs of moderating wage demands. The reasons for industrial unrest and what seems like extortionate wage demands, despite the Social Contract, has to be seen by people outside of Scotland against a background of some politicians seeking a statutory incomes policy, by implication a wage freeze; generalised statements that Scottish workers are worse paid than their colleagues in England; that there is a lower standard of living than in Europe; the demand of catching up on what had been lost during the three stages of the Prices and Incomes Policy introduced by the Conservative Government; and that many people involved in the wage demands are low paid by any standards. But Forman admitted that the alternative to the Social Contract was chaos and near-anarchy. It was necessary for government, unions and employers to show that the Social Contract was relevant to the inflationary situation and to make clear the implications to everyone if the Social Contract failed.

Lord Balfour wondered if a payroll subsidy could be any better than the Regional Employment Premium which had been welcomed as a good idea, but which according to most manufacturers had not really been effective, while Lord Taylor thought that a payroll subsidy would provide "feather-bedding" and would, like REP, be a *disincentive* to achieving sound economic objectives. His argument was that in West Germany, which is surviving better than most countries through its efficiency, and could finance some of the oil deficits through accumulative balance of payments surpluses, is not in a low wage economy, nor has an economy which subsidised labour-costs, but has, in fact, higher labour-costs than the U.K. and a greater degree of investment and a greater degree of efficiency. Employers who were paid to put people on the payroll, he said, had a disincentive to take people off the payroll, and efficiency might depend on a greater degree of investment with less people. The aim of economic policy has to be to achieve a high degree of efficiency, and consequently, it would be better if taxation revenues were employed, not to subsidise the employment of labour, but to create greater flexibility in training labour to take advantage of new investment opportunities.

Taylor agreed with Jay about the dangers of spending one's way out of unemployment – reflating the economy to avoid a high unemployment rate. Sir Keith Joseph (the Conservative shadow Home Secretary), whom Taylor regarded as a much misunderstood person, had made the point that in spending one's way out of unemployment, by reflating and creating employment, the price might be a higher social evil – intensified inflation and balance of payments problems. But Taylor was concerned also about propagating the idea that the simple answer to competitiveness and restoring the level of investment is cost and profitability. To create an economic structure in which profitability is going to be encouraged would cause very serious problems for the trades unions to sell the Social Contract, in an area where the idea of the profitability of an industry did not really commend itself, in present class-war terms, to many sectors of the labour movement.

There is one area in Scotland where cost-effectiveness does take place, according to Michael Moran, Managing Director of an electronics company, in relation to the United States and the rest of Europe – the qualified and professional skills in the manpower industry. He saw the situation as providing a ray of hope for Scotland in an otherwise gloomy situation. Salary differentials exist of between 2 to 1 and 4 to 1 between the United States and the United Kingdom, and at least 2 to 1 between Europe and the United Kingdom. In relation to the specific class of manpower resource, exchange-rate adjustments, payroll subsidies and Selective Employment Tax would provide an additional bonus which would create a significant improvement on the present cost effect of manpower resource. In his opinion, Scotland would retain this specific advantage until

Scottish manpower across the board became cost-effective relative to the world manpower scene. He suggested the resource could be harnessed by certain manufacturing businesses re-assessing, where possible, the corporate objectives in terms of restructuring their operations, so that the real strands are those which are internationally competitive – resources of marketing, product development, industrial engineering, and product valuation.

The objective was to manufacture a package which could be reproduced anywhere, if necessary where the adjusted labour-costs were attractive and therefore capital available. Such a corporate strategy, if adopted on a meaningful scale, would help stem the outflow of the precious cost-effective talent from Scotland. There were already signs that the "brain drain" to Europe was starting to flow. Such a strategy, he claimed, would enable businesses to smooth out the economic "boom-bust" problems, by spreading their manufacturing base and, most important of all, locate the resources on the real cost-effective strength of the business.

He sounded one note of alarm. Cost-effective manpower originated primarily from the universities and colleges and there existed an alarming downward trend to its further supply. During the seven years 1968/73 the intake into British universities and colleges had increased slightly from 56,222 in 1968 to 61,914 in 1973. Those entering electrical engineering, however, fell from 2,204 or 3.92% of the total intake to 1,796 or 2.90%; in mechanical engineering over the same period there had been a drop from 1,775 or 3.16% to 1,310 or 2.13%; and in chemical engineering from 802 or 1.43% to 504 or 0.18%.

The postgraduate intake is also falling off at an annual rate of between 15–20%, and the situation of qualified technicians is even more alarming. One of the main reasons for the downward trend in this source of future talent was the steady erosion of their status and rewards in manufacturing industry. It is a microcosm of the national erosion of differentials that has taken place over the years, a sure recipe for inflation, because the cash is transferred in general from the savers and investors to the spenders.

Shipbuilder Sir William Lithgow agreed with Moran's view about human manpower, which next to oil was Scotland's most important asset and of which there had been a failure to make the best use. He was of the view that in the past ten years there has been too much generalisation, particularly when the maximisation and organisation of resources has been discussed. A failure of organisation led to poverty and he claimed that on Clydeside, as elsewhere in the country, there was a parallel between unemployment, enormous gaps, enormous breaks in the production chain and the misuse of manpower resources. Less than one-third, even a quarter, of unfilled vacancies are officially posted. In statistical terms there has been probably as much work, if not jobs, available as there had been unemployed people, almost continuously, since the end of World War II, and yet, time and again, because of generalisations by well-meaning people in the Scottish Council, in politics and elsewhere, brought up in the shadow of the Thirties, there has been an indulgence in reflationary policies without an understanding of the need to be selective, to get down to the individual problems. Problems broken down into their component parts are always soluble.

Inflation has been a particular problem of the shipbuilding industry for fifteen years, said Lithgow, and he took great hope from the fact that people, some of them up until a year previously had not regarded inflation as a threat, are now recognising that it is a terrible threat to democracy – a process which sets man against man, and most especially, worker against worker. Democracy, and the kind of freedom that the financial disciplines which people in Britain are used to, could only survive if the problems of inflation are grasped, and that meant recognising that "we cannot pay ourselves more than we are worth".

But recognising the problem of inflation is not enough, was Peter Jay's argument. He doubted whether on the one hand it was as fully recognised as Lithgow had said, or as little, by the workers as Forman suggested, when he had said that the Social Contract had not been "sold" as relevant to the problem of inflation.

"I do not think that just recognising the nature of the problem of inflation and the relevance of a mechanism like the Social Contract is by itself enough," emphasised Jay. "An organisation of society has to be created, and organisation of industry in which it is possible and in which it makes sense for the individual to move from the understanding that, for example, pay settlements in excess of productivity-growth causes inflation on the national scale, to being able to say to himself: 'It makes sense for me and my family and my shopfloor and my particular group of workers to restrain themselves.' It is not the case that the mere recognition of the micro-economic facts provide, by themselves, a sufficient motive for individual behaviour."

In the absence of some collective leadership, individuals would maximise their individual chances. It is not enough just to create an understanding of the nature of the problem, but necessary to create an organisation, or society, for an active, collective leadership in which it made sense for each individual to act on that understanding – and this was the great importance of an incomes policy and a Social Contract.

Jay, in defence of his theory of a payroll subsidy, rejected any suggestion that it would lead to a situation of "feather-bedding", or propping-up old industries, or creating, through providing cheap labour, disincentives to industry to invest or become efficient.

He found extraordinary the idea put forward by Lord Taylor that, if labour was subsidised, it would lead to less investment and efficiency when the British economy, and particularly the Scottish economy, had for forty-five years suffered from labour being too expensive – through the fact that it had not all been used. At the same time, he admitted that there is a danger that, if labour became too cheap by the standards of international competitiveness, then the incentive to invest is removed.

But it was not desirable to have a situation where the in-

centive to efficiency and investment was very high, but because
labour was too expensive there was not any possibility of profit,
and therefore investment did not take place, unemployment
remained high and the area stagnated. Neither did he agree
that a payroll subsidy would lead to the ossifying of the industrial structure, propping up old jobs, inhibiting change.
That was only true if labour was subsidised *in situ* in industry
where it at present was located. That was the kind of thing
which governments had gone in for with the coal industry and
shipbuilding and in many other areas, where they had inter-
vened to subsidise or in other ways assisted in keeping labour in
the jobs it was in. A general payroll subsidy of the kind which
he had suggested is available to anybody employing labour in
the specific area and does not have the characteristics of the
other type of subsidy. The market forces would tend to shift
labour from low profitability to high profitability, from low
investment to high investment, areas. The subsidy was across-
the-board and wholly non-specific as between one industry and
another. Those industries which could not compete, even with
the benefit of the general across-the-board subsidy, would tend
to go out and give way to those industries which were more
profitable. It was Jay's opinion that the essence of the matter
is that a general environment would be created in which those
things which ought to be decided by entrepreneurs and not by
economists would be decided by the entrepreneurs. One of the
things which the entrepreneurs should decide – and not
economists – is which firms go up and which go down, which
should flourish and which should not.

What, then, was the difference between the payroll subsidy
and the Regional Employment Premium?

REP had four characteristics distinct from the payroll subsidy:

1. It was fixed in £.s.d. and not as a percentage of payroll and
was eroded by inflation. 2. It was selective, in that it applied
only to manufacturing industry and not to all employment in
the development areas, whereas payroll would be for all
employment in an area. 3. It was temporary, or believed by

industry to be temporary. Started in 1967, it was to run initially to 1974, whereas the payroll subsidy would be permanent. (The defect of REP was that it was supposed to change the basic cost structure of an area in order to create a new dynamism, but business people did not believe it to be a permanent change in their cost structure and therefore did not include it in their future investment planning to any great extent, with the result that its effectiveness was blunted.) 4. It was too small an amount.

But Jay did not regard REP as a total failure. The evidence suggested that 40,000 jobs, all in development areas, were created, although it was not as effective as had been hoped. A payroll subsidy would get results.

Combining profitability with the Social Contract was the $64,000 question – not only for the Scottish economy or the British economy, but for all industrial economies.

"It is a question which I think is coming more and more to the front and underlies more and more of our difficulties," said Jay.

It was not a question any technician – or even perhaps any human being – could answer. The situation might be fast approaching in which the minimum terms on which capital is able to operate are ceasing to be compatible with the minimum terms on which labour is prepared to participate in the economic process.

If capital and labour cease to combine, then for the basic textbook reasons, economic activity ends, which is disaster for everybody.

"Whether they come to see that in advance, or whether mutual suspicions and jealousies and anxieties, that somebody is going to put something over on somebody else, will have such hypnotic effect on people that those terms will remain incompatible, in which case labour and capital will no longer be able to combine, and economic activity will come to an end, is the most fundamental of all the economic questions facing all economies."

chapter 3

Oil
Dimensions

"If we survive the next seven years . . ." the medium-term future for Europe is hopeful because of its ability to energise itself through North Sea oil.

This rather ominous message was given by Professor Peter Odell, of Rotterdam's Erasmus University, where he is Professor of Economic Geography and Director of the Economic Geography Institute at the university.

Regarded by some people as the *enfant terrible* of the oil scene, Odell, a graduate of the University of Birmingham, had warned against the British Government's policy of reducing output from the coalmines in the early 1960s when Middle East oil was being produced at $1 a barrel, because he foresaw the end of cheap energy from oil while a lecturer at London School of Economics. His predictions, made through the studies which are being carried out at Erasmus University, that North Sea oil potential was up to five times greater than government forecasts have been criticised, but not by the oil companies. Two weeks after the Forum where Odell revealed the statistics, one of the critics, Lord Balogh, Minister of State at the Department of Energy, conceded during a talk with American businessmen that Odell's forecasts *in the past* had been generally accurate.

Odell, who bases his arguments about the need for change on the economic situation, is obdurate about the accuracy of the research he and his team have done at Rotterdam.

"If we survive the next seven years . . ." is the qualification to all that he says, because he is even more pessimistic about the economic situation for Western Europe than Peter Jay.

"There has been a revolution in the world economic order, and the revolutionary order consists of the fact that the western world has lost control over a part of that system, not just any old part of the system, but a very important part of the stuff, oil, that makes the wheels of the western world go round. The price of this commodity now lies entirely outside the hands of the traditional decision-takers in the western world and in the hands of people who are not used to exercising this authority and who have more motivations for using the power they now have to collapse the Western system than to see its continuity."

The short-term solution lay only in a deliberate austerity in the Western world as a means of achieving what Odell considers should be its primary aim – the break-up of the Oil Producing Export Countries (OPEC) cartel, to ensure the survival of the system. That also involved the acceptance of the idea of maximising Western Europe's own energy production, and energising the economy to the greatest possible extent as soon as possible. The historic trend of the last two decades in which Western Europe has become dependent upon a flow of essential energy from areas of other parts of the world has to be reversed. There has to be a return, after twenty years of accepting cheap external energy as a means of advancing the economic system, to a consideration of Western Europe having its own resource base as a means of ensuring the medium- to longer-term future of its economies.

He was despondent, however, that there is an attitude that nothing fundamental has changed in the world economic order and that the problem will go away of its own accord, without the need for sacrifices in the life-styles and living standards to which people had become accustomed.

It was not inconceivable, he admitted, that there could be events in the next few years which would prove to be as traumatic as those in the oil world since December 1970, e.g. a return to competition between the oil-producing countries, with an 80% reduction in the revenues they earned per barrel of oil produced. But most people would, quite justifiably in the light of present evidence, attach a very low probability to such a development. Some would not attach a much higher probability even to the idea of a slow but steady improvement in the security of supply and the price of OPEC oil, or to the possibility of the international oil companies increasing their influence on the decisions about how much oil should be produced. Sober and sombre realism would indicate that the present disadvantageous position of both oil companies and oil-importing countries in the world of oil power will continue to get worse given (1) the absence of any substitutes in the short- to medium-term, (2) the indifference of many oil producers as to whether they produce more oil or less, (3) the pre-disposition of some producers to see their control over oil primarily as a political weapon.

North Sea Oil

Scotland has an opportunity to make the most important contribution to the energising of Europe in the post-1980s, if Odell's predictions are correct, because the North Sea has become "activity centre number one" for the largest international oil companies.

But as Odell pointed out, the conversion by the oil companies to the North Sea has been a fairly recent one. The boom only started because of the justifiable pessimism over the world oil situation. From January 1971 until mid-1973, the international "majors" thought that their best interests lay in collusion with OPEC, whereby the consumer would be forced to pay (albeit quite modestly compared with what has happened since) for greatly increased revenues to the oil-exporting countries and for modestly increased profits to be taken by the oil companies.

In Odell's book *Oil and World Power* (Penguin, 1973) he argued that during the late 1960s moves took place among the companies to re-establish an international oil agreement – to protect profit in a situation where taxes would be increased by the producing countries. The United States legal restraints on such agreements, through the making of effective anti-trust legislation, was the main barrier. But after the overthrow of King Idris of Libya, the take-over of oil companies' assets by the Government under Colonel Gaddafi, along with the collective action of OPEC, the administration of President Richard Nixon was persuaded that there was a danger of a world oil crisis. In 1971 the go-ahead was given for the oil companies to take collective action.

Though the companies created the appearance of fighting OPEC tooth-and-nail over the agreements – as they sought to keep their increased tax obligations to a minimum and to delay participation in (that is, nationalisation of) their oilfield and other assets as long as possible – they certainly recognised that their best hopes of future profitability, and even survival, depended on successful co-operation with the major oil-producing countries.

The latter, in turn, initially accepted the idea that they needed to work with the international oil companies in order to keep the oil, and thus their revenues, flowing. Thus the OPEC/oil companies collusion became a fact of the oil-power system of the early 1970s – with the positive encouragement of the United States.

The U.S.A. wished, indeed, to see the establishment of a new collective stability in the oil system for two reasons. In the first place, it sought to provide a basis for a renewed effort to find a political solution to the Middle East conflict, arguing that higher revenues and a greater degree of economic certainty for the Arab oil-producing nations would make it easier for them to accept a compromise in their dispute with Israel, and so bring greater political stability to the whole of the Middle East.

Secondly, given the fact that the U.S.A. was fed-up with a situation in which the rest of the industrialised world had access to cheap energy (and which the U.S.A. itself could not have because of its underlying belief in a policy of autarchy in its energy policy), it deliberately initiated a foreign policy which aimed at getting oil-producing nations' revenues moving strongly up by talking incessantly to the producers about their low oil prices and by showing them the favourable impact of much higher prices. It was, of course, assured of the co-operation of the largely American oil companies in having these cost increases, plus further increases designed to ensure higher profit levels for the companies, passed on to the European and Japanese energy consumers, so eliminating their advantage over their competitors in the United States. And, in as far as the U.S.A. itself would be affected by the higher foreign-exchange costs of the increased amount of foreign crude oil that it expected to have to import, even this would be offset entirely, or to a large degree, by the greatly enhanced abilities of the U.S. oil companies to remit their increased profits back to America.

Thus, within the framework of a re-evaluation of how their best interests could be served and the consequential establishment of what might be termed a somewhat "unholy alliance" between the United States, the international oil companies and OPEC, the stage was set for changing the international oil-power situation as it had evolved over the previous fifteen years.

From the companies' point of view, of course, acceptance of the producing countries' terms on increased taxes and on the idea of participation (another device for increasing the share of the profits going to the countries) implied a major increase in their tax-paid costs. This meant that the weakness in the market places of the oil world had to be eliminated – as permanently as possible – if the companies were to earn what they considered to be adequate profits. The actual timing of the OPEC success and the companies' acceptance of it can, in fact, be correlated with the occurrence of a hardening of the oil-market situation in 1970, due to the combination of a set of unusual circumstances – a strong demand for most oil products in most markets in a period of general economic advance, a shortage of refinery capacity in Europe and Japan, and a temporary scarcity of tankers which was aggravated by the politically occasioned closure of the Trans-Arabian pipeline. The fact that oil prices strengthened as a result of this set of circumstances now gave the oil companies the public-relations opportunities to start to persuade oil consumers that there was an oil supply crisis – not only of short-term but also of long-term dimensions – and that this, coupled with the imposition of the "swingeing" new taxes in the producing countries, inevitably meant significant and continuing rises of oil prices over the foreseeable future. The U.S. energy crisis – certainly a real one, but nevertheless an essentially short-term crisis arising out of domestic issues – and the impact of the conservationists and the environmentalists, added further strength to the inevitability-of-higher-prices-for-oil arguments. And the public was persuaded of the oil companies' case!

The climate, in other words, was established for an attack on oil consumers' interests – with the elimination of the cheap energy (and essentially low-profit energy) to which Europe, Japan and elsewhere had, by 1971, become very accustomed. Temporarily, the factors mentioned above could be relied on to secure the situation, but their ephemeral nature meant that the safeguarding of the longer-term position required positive action on the part of the companies. Fortunately, their ability and new opportunity to work and negotiate together with the oil-producing countries gave ample opportunities for strategic marketing discussions – and for a decision to tackle the inbuilt propensity for price weakness in Europe. This market was the critical one, for it was to Europe in the past ten years that "distress" supplies had found their way in their search for outlets. The appropriate device to achieve this end was obviously a moratorium on the expansion of the infrastructure through which oil is moved and marketed in the Continent (particularly in refining and pipelining facilities), accompanied by some element of rationalisation in the complex company structure involved in the marketing of oil products in Europe. Thus, expansion projects were slowed down and some companies – for example, Gulf, Shell and BP – decided to pull out of certain national markets and/or products, whilst in the case of some products – for example, aviation fuels – there was evidence of an agreement that existing suppliers of particular customers were accorded the right to continue to have the business without the fear of price under-cutting by other companies. All this, of course, fell far short of the establishment of a formal cartel of oil companies – or even a repetition of the 1933 "As Is" agreement, under which the oil companies formally agreed to leave market shares, etc. as they were. However, given the understanding between the companies, and the fact that almost all of them were involved in the collective discussions which were required to reach agreement with the oil-producing lands, it promised to be enough to get some high degree of "sanity" and "orderly marketing" into the hitherto cut-throat and generally chaotic market situation in Western Europe.

At first, three factors combined to undermine the strategy (though it should, nevertheless, be noted that most oil prices in most countries did go up by more than enough to compensate the companies for the higher taxes they were having to pay in the producing countries and for other increased costs, with, of course, favourable effect on oil-company profit margins). In the first place, the weather was against the oil companies, for Europe had a series of warmer than average winters and this, of course, played havoc with the expected demand for heating oils. Likewise, demand for industrial fuels was less strong than expected because of the slow-down in the rate of European economic growth. The companies did, of course, recognise the likely temporary nature of these two factors and were thus prepared to "sit out" their influence.

The third factor, however, was potentially much more dangerous to the companies' strategy in that it threatened to get worse over time. This was Western Europe's newly found large-scale sources of natural gas, which, as the fuel preferred by most customers in a wide variety of end-uses, threatened to lead to stagnation in the growth of oil markets. However, though the factor threatened to get worse, it was, nevertheless, eminently controllable, in that most of the gas production in

Europe was undertaken by one or other of the international oil companies, which thus had the option – on the basis of some pretext or another – of ensuring that production was held back. This happened in both the Netherlands and the United Kingdom, where the future development plans for the expansion of the energy source were significantly restrained. It was assumed that the worst effects on the profitability of oil markets arising from the growth of the availability of natural gas would be over by 1974, when with average or worse than average winters, plus a resumption of industrial growth in the Continent, the increased demand for oil could be expected to lead to traumatic results as regards the prices for most products. And with the European market "under control", with orderly marketing replacing the competitive situation of the twenty years since the mid-1950s, the oil companies could reasonably further assume that markets elsewhere in the world would take care of themselves. The tax and cost increases in oil production, etc. could be more than passed on to consumers – with consequentially highly favourable conditions for higher profits.

In brief, the competitive nature of the oil market between the middle 1950s and 1970 has proved to be an aberration, in that we have since seen the scene set for a reversion to the more normal oil industry pattern of producer's control over the supply of oil. Until 1973, however, it was intended and accepted that this would once again be under the leadership and direction of the major international oil companies – even though they, in turn, certainly recognised that the greater part of the enhanced profits to be made out of the restrained supply situation would flow to the producing countries, whose interests, the companies thought, would thus be served to the full satisfaction of the countries concerned. Thus, the Teheran and Tripoli and other negotiations in 1971 and 1972 between the companies and the producing countries could be viewed as an attempt by producers – both companies and governments – to achieve a satisfactory *modus vivendi*, within the framework of which somewhat increased profits and greatly increased revenues, respectively, could be achieved. What the companies essentially had in mind was the establishment of orderly oil marketing in place of the chaotic and limited-profitability situation of the previous fifteen years.

The strategy depended not only on the producing countries' willingness and ability to work together – a development which was achieved through the increasing effectiveness of OPEC – but also on their continuing to accept the idea that the major oil companies had an essential role to play in the international oil industry. And this was not only in respect of their role in transporting, refining and marketing the oil, but also as decision-takers on fundamentally important matters such as levels of production and the development of producing capacity in different countries. In this respect the companies interpreted their responsibility as one in which the supply of oil was expanded more or less *pari passu* with the expectation of an average 8% per annum rate of growth in demand.

The grand strategy of the oil companies was completely undermined by the members of OPEC which, in 1973, simply decided to take control over the world oil industry. The companies lost the freedom they thought they had secured (by virtue of the Teheran and Tripoli agreements with OPEC) to be able to continue to take the essential decisions on the supply and price of oil on the world market until 1982 – as it was not until then that the oil-producing countries would have finally achieved a 51% controlling interest in the producing operations. During the eleven years the companies planned to serve the world's markets for oil out of reserves in OPEC, reserves which, in usual oil industry fashion, were significantly understated and which were sufficient, in reality, to ensure the world's oil demand for the period without having to worry about finding new and immediately produceable reserves in other locations.

By mid-1973 it became abundantly clear to the companies that they could not rely on another decade of freedom as far as OPEC oil was concerned (the renewed hostilities between the Arab States and Israel put the finishing touches to an already rapidly changing scenario). By January 1974 loss of control was only a matter of months. For the companies, dependence on the OPEC decisions as to how much oil should be produced completely undermined their ability to organise the logistics of the oil supply system around the world; whilst the likelihood that they would have to pay the posted or tax-reference price for crude oil to the exporting countries, for most of the oil they needed, undermined their abilities to make any significant profits out of the system! Given these developments, OPEC oil was becoming a supply of last resort to the companies concerned. The uncertainty over supply continues to be serious, and when the oil companies finally sell the last of the oil obtained at pre-crisis prices, their profits are likely to be decimated.

(Britain's twenty-fifth largest company, Burmah Oil, went to the Government at Christmas 1974 with the information that there was a cash crisis in the company. It was estimated that Burmah's borrowings had amounted to £400 million and that there was not enough money to pay the interest charges out of profits. Burmah had bought over the U.S. Signal Oil which had two large oil strikes in the North Sea. The company was not bankrupt, but had run itself into debts which were due for repayment and could not find the cash.)

The situation which has taken place with OPEC is highly relevant to Scotland. For it has been as a result of the traumatic changes in the fortunes and in their relationships with OPEC that the oil companies have re-ordered the development of the North Sea to the topmost priority – not simply because they need the North Sea to provide a guaranteed supply to Western European markets, but also because it seems likely to be the oil production on which they will be able to make the most attractive profits.

What had been, until 1974, intended by the oil companies as a rather leisurely and modest exploration and development programme in the North Sea (in order steadily to prove a productive capacity which after 1980 could be converted into actual production as a substitute for the declining availability of owned crude from OPEC) has now been turned into a search and exploration effort in which the emphasis has become one of as much oil as possible, as quickly as possible.

The essential question in trying to evaluate the likely flow of oil investment into Scotland, because of the fundamental shift in the oil companies' attitudes to the significance of the North Sea, and because of a similar, though much more modest, European reaction to the opportunities presented in the potential of substituting indigenous for imported energy is:

How fast can the exploration and exploitation effort be built up?

(The question does not take account of any view of the environmentalist, the conservationist, or the Government's policy on British energy needs – see Chapter 4.)

According to Odell, it can be assumed that all the companies with an interest in the North Sea would behave as though all the oil that can be found will not only have a ready and waiting market in Western Europe, but would also be marketable at a higher rate of profit than that which could be achieved on any alternative way of supplying oil to the Continent. The prime input, therefore, with any investigation of the future of Scotland's involvement with oil investment had to be a realistic forecast of the likely rate of exploration, of the associated rate of likely discovery of reserves and of the production potential to which these reserves gave rise over time. All official forecasts have failed to present a reasonable view of future developments for two reasons: 1. Inadequate interpretative ability about what is happening – perhaps not surprisingly, given the general degree of unfamiliarity with resources development after a generation in which successive governments have either discounted or ignored the role of natural resources in development or even seen them as representing a positive handicap to soundly based economic growth; 2. The interpretative ability which exists is still in the process of trying to catch up with the traumatic events of 1974 in the world of oil and is only belatedly recognising the importance for the North Sea's development of the joint impact of greatly increased prices for foreign oil and the rising degree of uncertainty over its availability. (The oil companies, though more aware of the revolution in the world of oil, have either been too busy to accept their responsibilities for informing governments and people of the North Sea potential, or else have had very good reasons for keeping quiet, perhaps for fear of environmentalists or socialist reactions to their plans.)

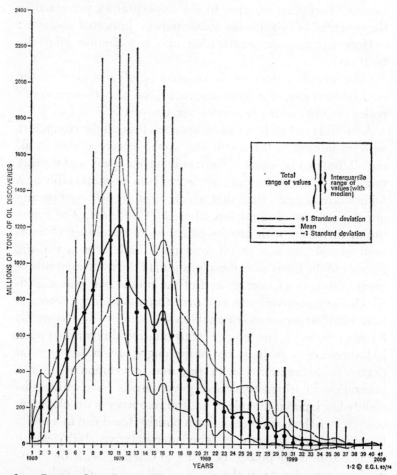

fig. 1 Ranges of year-by-year discovery and appreciation of North Sea reserves from 100 iterations of the model.

Potential Odell and his colleagues in Rotterdam decided because of the failure of official forecasts to present a reasonable view of future developments, to redouble their efforts in building a simulation model of the long-term potential for North Sea oil production. The initial stages of the work were completed just before the International Forum took place, and some

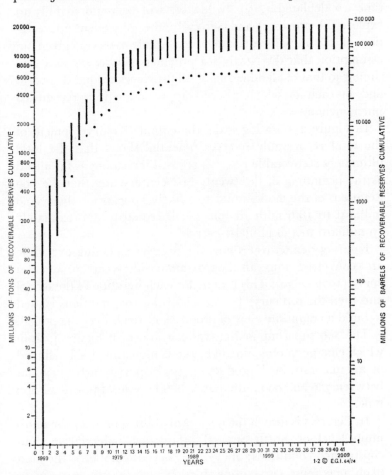

fig. 2 The cumulative development of the North Sea reserves. The vertical line for each date shows the range of the reserves volumes produced by 99 iterations. The 100th iteration is shown separately. It lies well below the general range as it emerged from an iteration in which the early exploration efforts "failed" and led to a diminution of exploration activity by the companies.

of the more important conclusions of the work were presented (the completed version of the initial stages was published in December 1974 in the *Journal of Energy Policy*).

Figure 1 illustrates the 100 simulations of the amount of oil added to reserves each year on the basis of, firstly, an assumed twenty-year primary exploration phase (during which time a calculated 1,650 "wildcats" will be required fully to explore the province) and, secondly, the subsequent appreciation of the initially declared recoverable reserves, given an assumption that the North Sea province will behave in a way similar to that of all other major oil provinces around the world and in each of which reserves-appreciation is a recognised phenomenon.

In Figure 2, on a log scale, the cumulative development of the total recoverable reserves potential shows that the total ultimately recoverable reserves are still increasing as far ahead as the beginning of the twenty-first century and that the 100 iterations of the model indicate a likely range from about 10.8 milliard to 18.9 milliard tons of oil (equal to approximately 79 milliard to 138 milliard barrels).

Figure 3 demonstrates how the reserves emerging over time are converted into an approximate fifty-year production curve (1972–2022). This is done for each iteration of the model and then the top curve from each of the 100 iterations is used to build a composite view of production trends over the period.

The 100 superimposed curves are shown in Figure 4, from which emerges a bunching of forecasts indicating the likelihood of an unconstrained production peak in the early 1990s at between 750 and 900 million tons of oil a year (15 to 18 million b/d).

In Figure 5 is drawn the 90% probability curve for the minimum level of North Sea oil production potential in non-constrained conditions: above this curve is computed the most likely maximum curve of production such that the two curves show the evaluation of the most likely range of production potential which could be achieved from the North Sea – if such high levels of production in the 1980s and the 1990s were

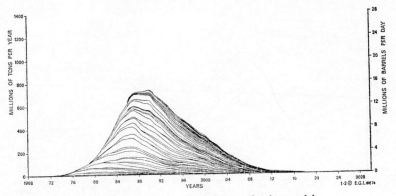

fig. 3 An individual iteration of the North Sea production model.

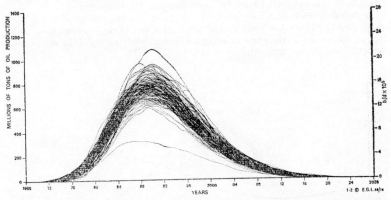

fig. 4 100 iterations of the production model. The quite separate production curve emerging from the "failed" exploration efforts (see fig. 2) also stands out clearly in this diagram – this, of course, represents the 1% probability of a curve of total production from the North Sea as low as this.

considered appropriate at national and/or European levels.

However, as shown in Figure 6, the mean curve of production potential rises strongly above 75% of the expected demand for oil in the whole of Western Europe for almost the whole of this period, suggesting that constraints on production might well be appropriate, even within the geographical context of this large energy-intensive using region, in order to extend the availability of North Sea oil well into the twenty-first century.

The model, as it has been developed to date in Rotterdam,

67

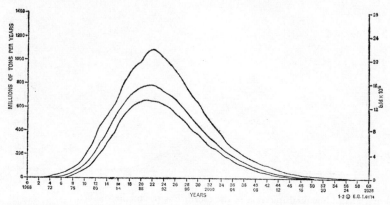

fig. 5 Production potential from the North Sea province 1969-2030.
The mean shown is that between the lower curve (i.e. the curve indicating the
90% probability level of total annual production not being less than this) and
the upper curve (i.e. the curve showing the highest likely values of the minimum
production level per annum).

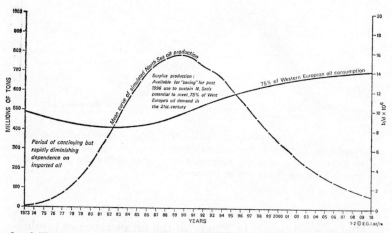

fig. 6 The mean curve of simulated North Sea production potential compared
with 75% of expected Western European demand for oil.

does not yet differentiate between the different parts of the
North Sea province, but this is an aspect to which we are now
turning our attention. Eventually it is hoped not only to be
able to simulate the potential from the various national sectors
of the province, but also that from particular geographical

locations, such that the results will provide guidance for the planning of pipeline networks and of on-shore installations – and hence help in forewarning of potential environmental dangers, as well as in the planning for the availability of appropriate social and economic infrastructure in the locations where expansions of oil-based developments appear probably to be required.

Until this work has been completed, however, it is only possible to relate the conclusions on the total potential of the North Sea province to Scotland in a tentative way – but, nevertheless, in a way which offers a more rational basis than hitherto for indicating the orders of magnitude of oil-related development in the Scottish economy.

The British sector of the North Sea province constitutes, as shown in Figure 7 (which is up-to-date to the end of September 1974), roughly half of the total prospective area for hydrocarbons; but most of that which is prospective for oil lies off the coast of Scotland in which waters, moreover, it is evident that many of the more prolific structures tend to lie. It would thus seem appropriate to hypothesise one-half of the total North Sea potential as being Scotland-related. On this basis Scotland ends up with possible total recoverable oil reserves ranging from $5\frac{1}{2}$ to 10 milliard tons (40 to 70 milliard barrels) and a potential annual rate of production rising to a peak in the early 1990s of at least 300 million tons and possibly as high as 500 million tons (6 mill. and 10 mill. b/d respectively). And, from 1976 to the peak production year, there would be a quite steady build-up in the levels of potential production indicating a development of capacity of between 20 and 30 million tons per annum.

Now these conclusions can, with sufficient effort – such as that already under way in the Department of Political Economy in Aberdeen or in the sort of programme that Strathclyde will presumably be starting in its new Institute for the Study of the Scottish Economy – be converted into terms of the consequent potential flow of investment into Scotland and associated development, such as the creation of new jobs and new in-

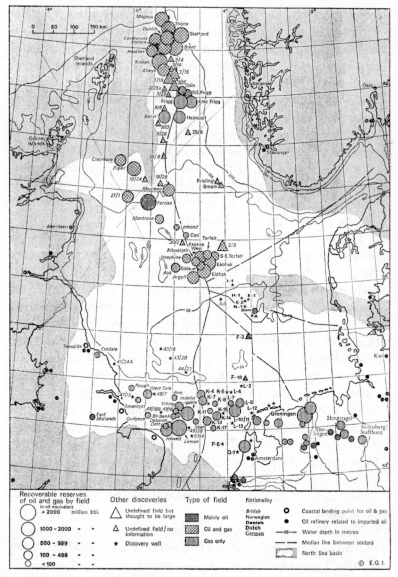

fig. 7 The North Sea oil provinces discoveries up to September 30, 1974.

dustries. And similarly, the research team in the Geography Department at Aberdeen could use this kind of input in their studies of the impact of oil on the environment – and there will, of course, be no need to persuade businessmen, institutional investors and others of the size of the opportunities for development that such a potential oil sector of the economy engenders.

To all such parties it will be obvious that this interpretation of the potential oil dimension to investment in Scotland's future is both larger (by several magnitudes) and much longer-lasting in its significance than previously indicated – a difference which one would claim, perhaps, emerges out of the first serious scientific attempt to look at the overall prospect for development in the light of the international oil and the European economic situation, as well as out of a dynamic appraisal of the oil province's long-term potential.

Impact on Scotland

Accepting the potential as indicated, what impact will it have on Scotland? And does the Scottish economy have the ability to sustain the pace and scale of the indicated required development?

Odell thought that there were two aspects to the latter question. Firstly, the absorptive capacity of the Scottish economy which he presumed was a yet-unstudied subject, because of what appeared to be the generally accepted view "that the oil development will still leave the economy in need of strong assistance from a regional policy and from other sources which offer a possibility of growth".[1] The view, he maintained, is related to the hitherto more limited interpretations of the pace and quantum of oil development. The levels of oil potential – as presented by Odell and his colleagues – necessitate a re-thinking of the conclusion, even in terms of the total Scottish economy, and much more so in terms of the regions of Scotland where oil-associated activities were going to be concentrated.

There is also some doubt as to whether enough consideration

[1] L. C. Hunter and G. C. Cameron of Glasgow University, in their paper to the British Association at Stirling, September 1974.

has been given to the scale of possible forward linkages into other activities, arising out of the availability of large quantities of crude oil on the east coast of Scotland and in the Orkneys and Shetlands. In terms of oil refining, petro-chemical developments and other energy-intensive industries (which could also be based on the even less well-studied availability of associated gas from the oilfields) there would be several conflicting locational forces at work to stop the developments because of fears for the environment, and the pre-existing structure of industry. Effective opposition to the industrialisation would keep the multiplier effect to a minimum. Another powerful set of forces pulling generally towards the same end are those in favour of transporting the oil and gas to pre-existing refining-processing and energy-using locations in England and other parts of Europe, and where oil from Scotland will either simply substitute previous energy inputs from other sources, or be used to energise the further development of geographically-concentrated activities in the already industrialised locations. It could be argued that most of the oil companies with large-scale production potential from the North Sea already under development would have a preference for moving the oil to their existing refineries, e.g. by 1980 it could be expected that the Shell, Esso and BP refineries in Rotterdam would be working mainly on North Sea oil. As far as these companies are concerned, commercial freedom to do what they like with their oil would only lead to a decision for major resource-based refineries in Scotland, if and when there is need for extensive new capacity in the total Western European context. Given the fall in Europe's oil demand, the existing surplus of refining capacity and the now expected reduced rate of growth in oil demand, it could be a decade or more before Scotland could reasonably expect a large amount of investment in new refinery and associated development based on the availability of oil from the North Sea. (In December 1974 Eric Varley, Secretary of State for Energy, in reply to a question in the House of Commons about the Government's policy on U.K. refinery capacity, indicated that there would not be a need for new refineries beyond those existing and planned. Refining capacity in the U.K. in the 1980s would be about 150 million tons a year – the equivalent of the Government's estimate of North Sea production.)

As far as the associated natural gas in concerned, the Gas Corporation will feed it into the national grid for the total British market, even though within the next ten years about two-thirds of the country's much expanded supply of gas would be coming in through Scotland – but there was no price discrimination in favour of the areas of origin (a policy which was taken as a result of Scottish Gas Board opposition to regional tariffs based on location, relative to the sources of supply in the mid-1960s, when gas supply points of origin were in Norfolk and Lincolnshire).

A third set of forces was also at work. It not only accepted the validity of oil- and gas-related industrialisation in appropriate parts of Scotland, but also wished to see policies pursued which sought to strengthen the economic case for resource-based locations for such developments. Shell, Esso and BP might be *pressured* into choosing such locations, but the greater hope for action lay in a requirement for such investment on the part of those companies unencumbered by previously developed locations in North Western Europe, so that they did not have to forego the advantages of expanding *in situ* when compared with the higher development costs at a new location. Another possibility lay in the establishment of a Scottish-based enterprise (whether in the public or private sector, or a mixed enterprise, is irrelevant) for refining, processing and using oil and gas in appropriate locations in Scotland – with the development made possible by a requirement on oil-producing companies that they needed to deliver to the enterprise as much crude oil and natural gas as it needed, at prices no higher than the transfer prices used when supplying these resources to sister companies of the producers.

But could Scotland raise or attract the massive flows of funds required for the development of the oil sector of the economy and its associated possibilities?

Odell believes that it can – from Europe, by using a closed system which would guarantee oil supplies from the North Sea.

"In these inflationary and generally unstable days of the Western capitalist system, the uncertainties about returns and tax rates are becoming so powerful, that even the most sophisticated evaluations made are being increasingly recognised as providing decreasingly valid bases for decision about any situation which remains open to uncontrollable external factors. Instead, there is increasing interest by investors – both private and state – in closed systems; systems that are so isolated from the external uncertainties that there is a guarantee of survival – if not of profit." (Except, of course, in the still largely, though not entirely, discounted possibility of the demise of the Western system.)

In this context it can be suggested that the time and the place, as well as the commodity concerned, create conditions for the establishment of a closed system around North Sea oil for the next fifteen to twenty years. It would put Scotland (and Norway) in an entirely enviable position *vis-à-vis* the rest of Europe. Scotland (and Norway) would soon have what the rest of Europe wants – a secure supply of large quantities of relatively low-cost energy. There would be no difficulty, therefore, in Scotland achieving the total capital flow it considered that it needed – and more besides. But success demanded an outward-looking Scotland, towards the prolific resources of the North Sea. It might be "Scottish" oil, but it could only be developed with Europe's money and it only had a value as long as European governments and users were prepared to buy it. It was this complementarity of interests which provided the basis for what could be one of the most important European agreements ever made – a long-term contractual arrangement to sell all the oil that can ever be produced out of Scottish waters, at a price related to the long-term supply price of the oil, plus a significant inflation-indexed economic rent for Scotland, in exchange for guaranteed markets, irrespective of what happened on the international oil scene, in those European countries prepared to participate in the project. Those countries would be required to raise, either through public funds or private interests, as much capital as was required for the oil and gas and all associated developments with which Scotland decided it wanted to go ahead; and with the payment of the interest and the repayment of the capital to be made out of the value of the ultimate flows of crude oil, oil products, natural gas and chemicals which were achieved from the resource development.

Security of energy supply, at a price which would be known not to make European energy relatively more expensive than it is at the present day, would enable the European countries concerned to plan much more effectively for their futures than is currently the case. For Scotland there would be the guarantee of development arising from the necessary flow of funds, which would make possible over the shorter term, and over the longer term, the guarantee of markets for all the oil and gas and associated products – even in a situation in which OPEC disintegrates, so that cheap oil from places like Saudi Arabia started to find its way on to European markets at prices which, in terms of current values of currencies, were no higher than the $1.50 per barrel of the period up to 1970. Such a development, if it occurred, would quickly undermine a non-guaranteed Scottish off-shore oil industry, so that few companies would remain interested in the continuation of production, let alone of development.

The amount of production of North Sea oil required to supply 75% of Western Europe's demand for oil would be about 300 million tons a year (double the highest British Government estimate but 200 million tons less than the potential indicated by Odell's model). Odell estimates that the total investment required would be about £500–£600 million a year, of which half would be provided by the companies themselves and the rest supplied by the institutionalised system of raising money. It might be a formidable amount for Scotland, but only amounted in Western Europe to just over £1 a head per year for the population of 250 million.

The limited financing operation would not only provide the

necessary means for raising the investment required in the future of Scottish oil but also serve to secure the economic and perhaps the political well-being of Western Europe, by isolating it from the uncertainties of a dependence on energy from other parts of the world.[1]

1 In February, 1975, the EEC countries agreed to a "floor" price of $7 a barrel in the future. The US had suggested $9 a barrel.

chapter 4

Oil
Future

The figures of potential oil reserves in the North Sea as forecast by Odell and his team at Rotterdam, if correct, could lead to an almost total re-thinking of the economic situation – and particularly the position of Scotland – by the British Government. A detailed study of the findings is undoubtedly being made, though the attitude is still one of scepticism.

By contrast, the oilmen do not disagree with the findings, and in turn are critical of the forecasts put out by the Department of Energy which shows a tapering off of activity in the North Sea by the mid-1980s, to no-activity by the early 1990s. (See diagram p. 82.)

On one thing both Odell and the Government agree – the estimates for production around 1980 from the U.K. Continental Shelf will be up to 150 million tons, with the Norwegian sector producing 50 million tons. But (as the figures in Chapter 3 show) Odell sees the level remaining high for twenty years beyond, a view which the Government is not ready to accept or commit itself on at this stage.

Gavin McCrone, Under-Secretary and Chief Economic Adviser at the Scottish Office, highlighted the difference:

"It is fairly clear that there is big disagreement between Professor Odell and other people as far as the future beyond 1980 is concerned. The way in which this has arisen is that Professor Odell's analysis is really based on the assumption that the thing will turn out to be much bigger than anybody expects, just because that is what always happens, and that if you apply the appropriate sort of uprating which was right for other cases – other cases were always discovered – to the North Sea, then you step the whole thing up by a very substantial amount. If one is going to put forward figures as a basis for investment, of one sort or another, whether by companies or public authorities, one does really need to get this more firmly established."

McCrone's view was that there were two types of figures which could be produced – the kind the Government produce in which there is a fair amount of confidence that they will be met (though he admitted that the Government had been wrong about the amount of natural gas in the southern North Sea – the estimates were too high); and those which are an intelligent guess and are extremely interesting but not of sufficient firmness on which to base public investment. However, if Odell was right, then it changed the nature of so many matters which were being considered in Scotland. At the same time, the gloom which Peter Jay and other economists shared about the short-term situation, the higher energy prices many countries in Western Europe would be paying, with huge balance of payments deficits up to the 1980s, would not be so worrying. The situation would not be altered up to 1980, but it would provide a much longer time to pay off the debts which is a fundamental matter. Oil production at a rate higher than the predicted Government figure of 150 million tons a year would create the confidence of being able to cope with the debt situation in the long-term. At the same time, the higher figures would have a much greater impact on the Scottish scene than that which is being considered at present (the previous year, McCrone stated that North Sea oil would not be the panacea for Scotland's economic problems. It is a view he still holds, though he now admits that oil has had a greater impact than he thought possible).

Peter Gibson, director of the Offshore Supplies Office, part of the Department of Energy based in Glasgow, believed that the achievement of 100 million tons a year production from the North Sea by 1980 would be a major engineering feat by any standards. And he questioned Odell's projections, on the ground that the technology challenge in the North Sea was taking engineering ability to its limits, and that the economics of production were much more speculative than in the other oil-fields used by the Rotterdam team as examples.

Odell naturally does not accept the criticism levelled at his methods of analysis. In particular he defended his analogic approach, on which doubt was thrown by McCrone, by pointing out that it was the same approach constantly used by planners in respect of the other side of the economic equation – determination of demand in an economy (at an aggregated national level, at regional, and at sectoral level).

"We are prepared to accept the idea that the creation of a certain set of conditions, a certain level of new wealth in an economy, the creation of a certain distribution of wealth, the creation of a certain standard of living, will give rise to the demand for a certain set of goods and services," he argued. "Otherwise one can never use analogies from elsewhere, one can never use chained line extrapolation to produce results on which plans are often made."

The approach was used in many other aspects of national and regional development plans but was, in fact, less justified than using analogies available from other parts of the physical world to a new oil and gas province. The variables were by and large only physical and not human-social, which should be included in planning but were not.

Odell challenged his critics to show how the North Sea is unique – it has to be, if analogy cannot be used to draw experience from other parts of the world. At the university in Rotterdam the experience and analogies had been used very conservatively, compared to what had happened in other parts of the world.

The North Sea oil province is "unique" in respect of the demand conditions existing for anything that can be produced from it. There has not been, according to Odell, another case in recent history – perhaps in Texas or California in the 1920s – where it can be confidently assumed that every barrel of oil produced would find a market at a normal or at a super normal profit in the absence of Government intervention. The North Sea situation was the first time ever that a major oil-using region with the additional circumstances of political conditions made it necessary in the interests of all to produce the oil and gas, to get Europe away from the dependence on other parts of the world.

He was critical of the Government forecasts which showed oil production rising to a peak in the early 1980s and then declining to zero by 1992.

Support for this view was given by Bob Fox, managing director of Oil Exploration (Holdings) Ltd, who thought that the estimates, produced by civil servants bound by the hard facts presented, would make industrialists and financiers, not familiar with the oil situation, think twice about investing in it. An advocate of the Odell conclusions, Fox thought that they give people who wanted a little more flexibility in their policy planning more to think about than the Government figures. And he put the order of the magnitude of the North Sea figures into focus on a world-wide basis. The oil business had discovered in its history 900 billion barrels, of which 300 billion had already been produced and consumed.

"The interesting point about the offshore Continental shelves area – after the 1,000 ft of water depth – is that the potential oil or gas-bearing basin is one-third the landward area of a similar type of geologic basin, and in the last twenty years had yielded 200 billion barrels of the total. In the last twenty years we have added quite a lot to our oil inventory. The industry is moving very fast and moving faster off the shores of Scotland than anywhere else."

One aspect of the "tailing-off" prediction which concerned him is that there is an attitude growing about conserving the oil and this would cause a halt to developing the 1,000 wells needed to make a proper inventory of the North Sea.

"If industry feels there is going to be a restraint, going to be production controls, then there is not going to be the type of drilling required."

The Department of Energy in its "brown book" entitled *Production and Reserves of Oil and Gas in the United Kingdom,*[1] presented in May 1974, did appear hesitant about being too enthusiastic about the North Sea potential.

It stated: "Forecasts of future oil production must be subject to considerable uncertainty, since so much exploration remains to be done and since production has not even started. But the success of 1973 now allows a more optimistic view of the size of our reserves. Production in 1980, allowing for discoveries not yet made, could be in the range of 100–140 million tons. There is therefore now a very good chance that in 1980 we can produce oil equivalent to our demand. The likelihood of further discoveries both in areas already licensed and in new areas to be licensed later, opens up the prospect of reserves capable of sustaining production at the rate of 100–150 million tons a year, or even more, in the 1980s. These prospects again raise the question of how our supplies can best be used over time. Although the advantages from production at any level within this range would confer enormous benefits and last for a considerable time, they will not last for ever, and it is therefore especially important to make the best possible use of them.

"Since the first finds of oil in the Norwegian and the United Kingdom sectors in 1969 and 1970, there has been a complete transformation in the prospects for oil production from the U.K. Continental Shelf with ten discoveries having been declared commercial and many of the other promising finds already made likely to be commercial."

But the Department of Energy then went on to put up some qualifications. "Forecasting the level and time pattern of production remains, however, very difficult since it must take into account – how much oil exists in the reservoirs already discovered; what proportion of oil will be technically possible to recover; how many further *commercial* discoveries will be made and what is likely to be the extent of the recoverable reserves they contain; how quickly the oil can be brought ashore,

1 Production and Reserves of Oil and Gas in the United Kingdom: A report to Parliament by the Secretary of State for Energy: May 1974: H.M.S.O.

given the formidable technical and financial problems.
"No final estimates therefore can yet be given. The total
reserves and recovery factors of the discoveries already made
cannot be finally known until each discovery has been fully
depleted, although reasonably realistic estimates should be
possible for most fields when they have been producing for
about two years. Meanwhile it should be remembered that the
first oil from the United Kingdom sector is not due to come
ashore until later this year."

Author's note: no oil has been brought ashore by the end of 1974.

United Kingdom Continental Shelf Forecast Oil Production
Profile 1975-90

Commercial Discoveries and other Significant Finds up to 5th April 1974

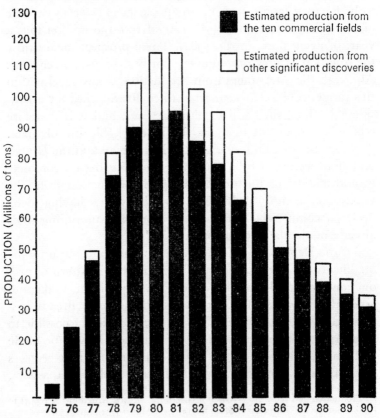

"Estimates of the number and nature of future discoveries are subject to a wide margin of error. Some promising geological structures have been identified in the areas still to be explored, but only drilling will tell whether they do in fact contain commercial oil deposits; and the timing of any such finds will depend very much on the scale of future exploration. The Government and industry are giving high priority to all matters affecting the timing of production. There are, however, many problems yet to be overcome; it takes time, for instance, to provide the necessary infrastructure, particularly in the remoter areas. Delays in building the production platforms for the first fields shortly to come on stream will probably delay the landing of oil in appreciable quantities until 1976."

Author's note: it is thought that this date will now be 1977.

"Certainly production in 1975 will not be as high as the level of 25 million tons forecast in the report published in May 1973. Although this slippage in the target for 1975 is disappointing, it is unlikely to reduce the production levels expected towards the end of the decade. Any forecasts of future production must therefore be very uncertain."

"On the evidence now available the significant discoveries so far made should contain enough reserves to support a minimum annual production of about 100 million tons over the period 1979–82. It is very difficult to forecast production exactly because of the time needed to construct all the facilities necessary to bring fields up to peak production. Production from existing discoveries is expected to fall below this level after 1982 and decline gradually thereafter as the peak production period of each field is passed, and the reserves begin to decline (in most cases, the peak production level is maintained for two to three years, after which annual production levels decline gradually until it is economically undesirable or technically impossible to extract more oil from the field).

"The estimates do not allow for the possible increase in reserves by uprating of existing discoveries, as they are further appraised, or by new discoveries. It is reasonable to assume

83

that there will be some increase in reserves on these grounds, but obviously very difficult to say exactly how big it will be. New discoveries are unlikely to make a large contribution until the end of the decade or later, since it takes 3–5 years to bring fields into production and a further 2–4 years for them to reach their peak."

Criticism was also made of Odell's proposal for a "closed system" in Europe. Alfred Matter did not think it would work, and hoped it would not be contemplated because it would be the beginning of the end. A re-thinking of the utilisation of the oil money in the Arab countries would be needed over the next ten years – the time Matter regarded it would take to recover from the crisis facing the "free world". A decision would have to be made about whether Europe and the United States took the Arabs on as partners, or convinced them on long-term investment, or some other kind of co-operative scheme. It would have to be done on a government level as well as on a private level, but government had always to try to put up the right conditions to let private enterprise work as freely as possible.

Peter Jay was appalled at the suggestion of a "closed system", which would be a return to the international trade and investment policies of the 1930s. There are already too many aspects of the economic situation which are reminiscent of that time, and the political implications of those economic characteristics, in terms of political disintegration and, ultimately, conflict between nations or great geographical groupings, are alarming enough without the addition of another analogy from the 1930s.

Trades unionist John Matheson did not think that the system was going to be of great benefit to Scotland, or Britain. It would certainly be of great benefit to Europe if it could depend upon a cheaper source of oil than the world markets. He was sceptical about investment being forthcoming from Europe, or that there is a future threat of a price-war with the Arab countries. Scotland would have an assured market without a "closed system" being set up in Europe.

Odell holds to his view – as he does over his estimates. Most of the investment required for the North Sea had been raised from American companies and people hoped it would continue.

He did not think it would, for two reasons: 1. It is not necessarily good for Western Europe to depend to that degree on the United States for the development of an indigenous resource – the U.S. does not like it and there could be a reaction against too strong an American intervention; 2. The United States has its own problems. Energy independence in 1980 would involve investment for the U.S. of £6,000 million in its energy industries, and much of the investment from American companies which might have been used to develop oil and gas in Western Europe would stay in the U.S. where it would be profitable and in American companies' terms secure. On that basis it would be necessary to provide not just a substitute for American capital but the additional amounts required within the framework of a more rapidly developing system. Neither was it a matter of *persuading* European investment, but rather creating a type of oil and gas investment bank in which individual Europeans could put their money, investing in a commodity which they used daily (Odell had coined the name **EPOC Ltd** – the European People's Oil Company).

Odell's theory of a "closed system" might or might not be feasible, or necessary, but there are other aspects of the North Sea oil development of immediate concern.

Sir William McEwan Younger, chairman of International Forum, who as the (now retired) chairman of the Conservative Party in Scotland had unsuccessfully attempted to persuade the Conservative Government of 1971–74 to revise its estimates on the potential which he regarded at the time as too low, warned that capital would not be raised unless there was adequate profitability. There is a real risk that if there is uncertainty about profitability, or returns are between 10 and 20%, as had been suggested, when the borrowing rate is at 15%, money would not be raised from Europe or anywhere else and that other areas – Alaska, Mexico and China Sea – would be given consideration.

85

Immediate, too, were the problems facing merchant banks like Morgan Grenfell (Scotland) Ltd. Director and manager, David Boyle explained some of the difficulties. Conventional, corporate financing solutions had provided much of the money for the early discoveries and there were still companies looking for these solutions. For many participants in oil discoveries, however, the size of the requirement of the companies in relation to their own resources poses an extremely large problem. They are looking for non-recourse or limited-recourse finance – for money the payment of which was not secured by their existing assets, but from the profits from sale of the oil providing the security. BP's Forties Field finance was an example, and though the only risk taken by the lenders was the absence of sufficient quantities of oil, the operating risk by BP was substantial. The Thomson Scottish Petroleum's share of the Piper Field (being operated by Occidental, Getty, Thomson and Allied Petroleum) was being financed on an extension of the principle, but the risks taken by the banks were more extensive, and the reward was correspondingly high. Some banks did not believe that loans of that kind were appropriate assets in which to place their depositors' money; other banks were prepared to make risk investments, but they would always represent a small proportion of the banks' assets. The international banking system had the capacity to make a number of financings with risks equivalent to Thomson's, but in the light of competing heavy demands over the next eighteen months on an under-capitalised international banking system whose new lending capacity would be constrained, not only by its lack of capital but by possible bad debts, it seemed most unlikely that bank finance would provide the whole solution to the North Sea's needs, even given the necessary profitability.

The ability of capital markets to meet any part of the needs would depend upon a more favourable climate for new private capital formation, both in terms of taxation and of increased certainty as to the returns available to investment. The returns had to substantially exceed the cost of money. Other sources of finance of field development might include off-take agreements from individual customers or, in some cases, National Import Agencies, on the lines of the Hamilton Brothers' deal with Texaco.

"I can only hope that beyond the next eighteen months Arab capital will become available in a form suitable to finance the North Sea field. If private sector financing is not available for oilfields the Government's determination to see the fields developed will lead to its offering its guarantee – but whether it would be enough is in doubt."

Iain Hope, a director of the insurance brokers Stenhouse, raised the problem which might face North Sea licence holders after the formation of the British National Oil Corporation. One-third of the current licence holders – the smaller and newer oil companies which were being encouraged two years ago – were finding it extremely difficult to raise finance, and it was difficult to foresee how they would fare under the pressures of the BNOC.

The British National Oil Corporation is being set up by the Government – the Petroleum Bill allowing the Government to do this is expected through Parliament by the summer of 1975 – to exercise participation rights in oil companies in the U.K. Continental Shelf. Discussions with the oil companies have taken place with a view to reaching a common interest which will continue to encourage the companies to invest in the North Sea on profitable terms.

BNOC is being set up because it is the Government's belief that majority State participation in the existing licences for commercial fields provides the best means for the nation to share fully in the benefits of North Sea oil, without unfairness to the licensees, with the State contributing its share of the costs, including past costs. The cost, according to some, of taking a 51% interest will be about £2,000 million.

In a White Paper[2] outlining the reasons for the BNOC proposals, the Government stated that participation in oil pro-

2 United Kingdom Offshore Oil and Gas Policy: A report to Parliament: H.M.S.O.

duction was the solution adopted with the consent of the oil companies in almost every other major oil- and gas-producing country in the world, and not just those in the Middle East. Public-sector participation had worked successfully in the British Shelf, without injury to oil-company interests, through the National Coal Board and British Gas, whose present shares would be accepted as a share in the total public participation. BNOC would, in fact, represent the Government on the consortia, and would take over the present interests of the National Coal Board. It is also anticipated that the BNOC would build up a powerful and expert supervisory staff (the number has not yet been decided, but one figure given is 1,500) that would enable it to play an active part in the future development, exploration and exploitation of the Continental Shelf. It would also have powers to extend its activities ultimately to the refining and distribution of oil. Though, to date, a location has not been decided for BNOC, it will be in Scotland – in Glasgow, Edinburgh or Aberdeen.

The Government's view is that with the expected production in the 1980s and the present high prices, the profits on Britain's offshore oil would be enormous.

Assuming the current price of oil, and on a realistic estimate of output, annual pre-tax profits would be about £4,000 million by 1980. Under the present system, tax and royalty would take a relatively small proportion of profits in the early years and would never take more than half. North Sea licencees would be in a position of reaping enormous and uncovenanted profits on their investments, with half or more of the post-tax profits going overseas – by 1980 the amount estimated is £1,000 million annually.

Much of the present Government's thinking on this had been influenced by the report of the Public Accounts Committee of the House of Commons under the chairmanship of Edmund Dell, M.P., now Paymaster-General. In December 1973 he complained that the then Government had not acted on the recommendations of the Committee which had pointed out nine months earlier that a great deal of revenue had been lost, and that the Government would not get the maximum benefit from oil because of a number of errors in granting licences and in the tax arrangements made with oil companies. The major fault in licensing policy had given the oil companies too easy a deal.[3]

In the White Paper the Government states: "Prominent leaders in the oil industry themselves accept that a more equitable arrangement is essential."

The Government therefore have two main objectives in the proposed Petroleum Bill:

– to secure a fairer share of profits for the nation and to maximise the gain to the balance of payments. This must mean a big increase in Government revenue from the Continental Shelf. On the other hand, the oil companies must have a suitable return on their capital investment; the Government recognise that the costs of exploration and development have been very heavy.

– to assert greater public control; this is essential if the Government are to safeguard the national interest in an important resource which belongs to the nation.

Apart from setting up the British National Oil Corporation, action will also be taken on the following:

Legislation to impose an additional tax on the companies' profits from the Continental Shelf, to close various loopholes in the rules governing existing taxation on the companies' profits.

It will be made a condition of future licences that the licensees shall, if the Government so require, grant majority participation to the State in all fields discovered under those licences. This will broadly follow the "carried interest" pattern successfully developed in Norway, under which the State has an option to acquire ownership of a specified proportion of oil or profits, meeting the same proportion of costs.

The Government will extend their powers to control physical production and pipelines. Experience has shown that there are many weaknesses in the current system. The Government will,

3 *Scotland's Goals*, p. 65: Jack McGill: Scottish Council/Collins.

therefore, for current as well as future licences, take power to control the level of production in the national interest. This does not affect their determination to build up production as quickly as possible over the next few years. The question of reducing the rate of depletion is unlikely to arise for some years, but the Government believe that they should take the necessary powers now. They will also take powers to receive royalty in kind, and to remit royalty in certain circumstances; to control the development of undersea pipelines, in the same way as on land; to introduce tighter control over exploration and development; and to require licencees to provide more information about their activities than is now obligatory.

All these new proposed powers, together with existing powers, will enable the Government also to ensure that development is carried out with a proper care for the environment and for the planning of infrastructure. The detailed implementation of these and other changes will be discussed with the companies.

Investment manager Peter de Vink of Ivory and Sime regarded the BNOC proposal as protectionist tinkering, which had a historical record of rendering industries ex-growth. To attract finance, the British National Oil Corporation had to allow a reasonable rate of return.

Whatever the outcome of the discussions and arguments between the Government and the oil companies, and the views of the bankers and investment managers, there is undoubtedly a great deal of "spin-off" from North Sea oil benefiting Scotland. Bruce Millan, Minister of State for Scotland, saw the discovery of oil as undoubtedly creating a radical change in the whole of Scotland's industrial and social future. It had taken some time for the Scots to come to terms with what oil could mean, and the opportunities it could offer – some opportunities had been missed in the past because of an unsteady realisation that they were there – considering that drilling had been going on since 1967 and the first declaration of a commercial oilfield made at the end of 1971. The most obvious opportunities were those for Scottish industry to participate in the large and lucrative market for the supply of goods and services for the exploration and production programme. Whether Odell's predictions were accepted, or something less optimistic, it had become increasingly clear that the off-shore market was neither a short-term nor a local phenomenon.

Even possibly more significant than having oil production off Scottish shores was the situation whereby production of oil from off-shore fields generally was projected to play an increasingly important part in meeting the world's oil needs, and there was the opportunity for Scottish industry to participate in the growing world-wide market. The Government was doing all it could to assist British, and particularly Scottish, industry to take advantage of the opportunities. It had been for this reason that the Offshore Supplies Office had been set up to sponsor and assist the establishment of a strong British-based off-shore supply and contracting capability. The OSO aimed to ensure that British industry was given a full and fair opportunity to compete for business in the U.K. sector of the Continental Shelf. It was also helping to identify areas of activity which offered opportunity for further technological development, and as oil production progressively moved into deeper waters, both in the North Sea and in other parts of the world, OSO would encourage British industry to be able to meet the new challenge.

Important market opportunities were available to British firms, particularly in the construction of production platforms and their associated equipment. The Government's policy was to ensure that British firms took a large share of the platform market, which would bring with it a greater chance of involvement in associated activities such as the construction of decks and modules. There were now more than 500 companies in Scotland which were known to have secured work connected with North Sea oil. Scottish industry was becoming aware of the opportunities and sharing fully in them.

The advent of oil has also led to an important expansion in educational and training facilities in Scotland and these developments are taking place across the board, from universities and central institutions to further education and the skill-centres of the training services agency. New courses are being devised and taught at existing institutions and some major training centres are planned.

Two of those are for drilling technology and for deep-sea diving, both of which are being located in Scotland. The drilling technology centre being set up by the Petroleum Industry Training Board is being funded by the Manpower Services Commission and it will provide specialised courses for drilling technologists and rig crews.

In an optimistic vein, perhaps it will be justified in the long term, even when compared to the events which have happened since, and the general gloom of the financiers, Millan said:

"Offshore oil exploitation is not limited to the North Sea. The continuing basis of expertise in the oil business which will be secured by developments will assure Scotland of an important role in the continuing development of offshore oil around the world."

chapter 5

Public
Investment

Public expenditure in Scotland now runs at well over £2,000 million a year – over a third of the gross domestic product – with public investment taking approximately a quarter of that figure – about £500–£600 million.

The agencies making these investments from the source of funds (central government provides a much higher proportion of the funds than it controls directly) are local, now regional, authorities, about 55%; public corporations (the nationalised industries) 25%; and central government 20% (including capital investment in the new towns and in housing by the Scottish Special Housing Association). The estimate of investment does not include incentives to invest as part of the regional policy, which comes out of current expenditure by central government. The amount can vary substantially depending both on the state of the economy and on the legislation in force. The possible cost in 1973–74 is £150 million, making the total for public investment in Scotland between £650–£750 million.

A very broad picture of the decision structure within which decisions about the investments are taken is that the regional authorities determine 45% of it, the public corporations 20%, the private sector another 20%, with perhaps one-third of this (6–7% of the total) selective assistance with government sharing in the decision taking, and about 15% of the total investment decided primarily by government itself.

Kenneth Alexander, Professor of Economics at Strathclyde University, Glasgow, examined some of the issues of principle (or theory) which arise in the taking of public investment decisions, against the background of Scotland's needs and opportunities – issues which span economic, administrative policies and social policy, and are of particular interest when the form of the government of Scotland is changing and a new agency (Scottish Development Agency) concerned with development policy is under discussion.

The scope of public investment, pointed out Professor Alexander, is very wide and the activities embraced extraordinarily diverse – opera house, operating theatre, bus shelter, pillar box, pier, palace, council house, container depot, ferry boat, motel, university building for business school, sports stadium, runway, power station, steel mill, tractor, power saw, crane. He was concerned with economic objectives and social objectives which include capital investment in education (over £20 million in the financial year 1972–73) as well as in nationalised industries. In addition, public investment includes the aid of one kind or another given to firms in the private sector, regional development grants, selective assistance, support for firms under legislation other than the Industry Act (1972), and in particular shipbuilding, as well as support for investment in agriculture.

The emphasis on decision-taking about investment is misleading, in so far as at any moment of time a substantial proportion of the investment is committed or in what might be called an "inflexible pipeline", so that pure decision-taking which might actually change the allocation of resources affects a lesser amount. A considerable – but unknown – proportion of investment is replacement of outworn or unsatisfactory capital. Whereas the replacement of such unsatisfactory capital can never be regarded as inevitable there are at least two reasons why in the public sector many existing investments tend to be replaced automatically, and therefore lie on the periphery of what might be regarded as the area of genuine decision-taking.

The first reason relates to the nature of the services which many of the investments contribute to – housing, education, health, transport and the like. Patterns and levels of need change, but there is much more historical continuity in the process of meeting such needs than there is in most of manufacturing industry, and the difference is accentuated by the much more unstable market situation which competition creates in the manufacturing sector.

The other reason for the continuity was, that even when such replacement investment may not be justified in terms of need and "consumer demand" there can be powerful sectional interests who favour it and are able to exert some influence in its favour because the decisions were taken in institutions subject to political influence and pressure. This is a central factor affecting public sector investment.

Even replacement investment involved decision-taking. Even in the provision of such goods and services, the form to be taken by capital goods being replaced involves choice and decision-taking. The number of houses may not be capable of much variation, but the square footage per house may. Replacement, with the question of location open, clearly involves decision-taking and much of the regional exhortation and policy has been aimed at keeping the question open and encouraging new locations for old activities. The timing of the creation and bringing into use of a new piece of capital equipment is, of course, part of the total decision involved. In the public sector, timing is affected more by political factors and directly by government policy than in the private sector. Investments are postponed or brought forward, according to how it is thought this would sustain the macro-economic policy at a given time. The use of public sector investment as a drag anchor or a pump primer, as a policy instrument in "stop-go", has been much criticised, but its avoidance seems unlikely.

Public investment, therefore, is substantial, diverse, rather inflexible in terms of the uses to which it is put, but frequently sensitive to changes in government economic policy.

Decisions about public investment are made by a range of very different institutions, consequently it is not a homogenous sector of investment activity or use, within which it is practicable to consider substantial switches between main sectors. Even the possibility of switching between sub-sectors within main sectors is not great, because of the replacement and "inflexible pipeline" aspects. A major expansion in one sub-sector e.g. the £600 million investment programme announced by the National Coal Board, is more likely to come from an expansion of public investment than from a switch within the fuel and power sector or even the wider public corporation sector.

Though obvious, Alexander stressed the point, because critiques of public investment policy often appear to be based on the proposition that because so much of the total money invested in the public sector is under the control or powerful influence of the Treasury, it ought to be possible to apply rather rigorous tests to its allocation and re-allocate it when the tests suggest that economic rationality would be better served by such re-allocation. Treasury officials, said Alexander, sometimes seemed to think that this is the position.

Allocation patterns can be changed, but slowly, and the period required might exceed the period for which the economic and social factors calling for the particular re-allocation exert their particular influence. Political circumstances change, so that re-allocations decided upon for economic and social reasons, fortuitously compatible with political factors at a given time, may run counter to political factors shortly afterwards, although there has not been a material alteration in the economic and social considerations.

Difficulties

What is investment in the public sector trying to achieve? Without a clear objective how can criteria be evolved for decision-taking and the making of judgments of actual decisions? The answer, according to Alexander, was "maximising welfare".

Ultimate judgments on welfare have to be made by public servants and politicians. But if society is open and democratic and the people well educated, actively interested in their own welfare and articulate, then the politicians were likely to adopt policies which came closer to the "wishes of the people" than if society is undemocratic and the people apathetic.

There is no analytical means by which the welfare of the people can be maximised, because that objective is the umbrella cover for a host of competing interests between which there is no scientific means for making infallible judgments.

Because of this unsatisfactory lack of analytical clarity affecting 40% of the total U.K. investments, several arguments are put forward as to what should be done.

Some economists argue that every aspect of public provision should be operated in such a way as to allow market tests to be applied; common standards of market demand and of costs of production reflecting market conditions would be applicable. There are a number of important qualifications to the view that such a market approach gives a sound basis for judging welfare ("best" allocation of resources and most efficient use of resources) stated Alexander. The most important of these qualifications arises from the existence of imperfect competition and monopoly, the impossibility, in practice, of firms responding quickly to the small, marginal changes in supply and demand as easily as theory assumes, and the existence of "externalities" i.e. costs and benefits which arise from the decisions of individuals and firms but are not reflected in their decisions because they are not borne by them. Setting these qualifications apart, however, the real difficulty and objection to using the markets as a means (either directly or by the use of "shadow prices" in calculations based, not on the situation of the public sector investor, but on a game of market make-believe) is that to do so overlooks the reasons why the particular activity was brought into the public sector in the first place.

Public goods, which, if they are supplied to all can be enjoyed by all without payment – because there is no way of denying people access to the goods – cannot have market tests applied. Local authority housing evolved as the only means which appeared to be available, to raise the housing standards of a substantial section of the population. The railways and mines were nationalised to secure a re-organisation of the supply of the service or commodity each produced, which it was thought would not come about as a result of market forces.

"It is not necessary for us to agree with these arguments for us to recognise that once an institution has been created to serve what is regarded as a social need because the market is judged as failing to serve it," said Alexander, "it is unlikely that the institution will take readily to the proposition that it ought to adopt market criteria in taking its decisions about investment and production. This is why it would be superficial to take too literally the tenor of economic and public policy statements on public sector investments in recent years with their emphasis on analysis and on commercial behaviour."

The evolution of the British system of management and control of public expenditure (and within it public investment) was set out by Sir Samuel Goldman[1] who had retired from the Treasury, and is used in Civil Service training programmes. He singled out the Plowden Report as making a decisive break with the system which had evolved from 1945–61.

Basically, the Plowden Report which was published in 1961 at the time of the financial and balance of payments crisis – an historical coincidence – recommended a system of long-term assessment, based on five-year "rolling" programmes for all departments of the Civil Service, covering the whole field of expenditure, and taking into account the medium-term prospects of the economy and the resources which were likely to be available to meet the demands of the public sector. Before the Report, three-year projects had been done on defence expenditure. The Treasury claimed that three-year estimating was standard procedure for all expenditure, but as Goldman points out "all who were then involved in these matters knew

1 Sir Samuel Goldman, *The Developing System of Public Expenditure, Management and Control.* Civil Service Department, H.M.S.O., 1973.

that the three-year estimates were on the whole regarded as something of a nuisance and engaged little of the attention of departments or the relevant divisions of the Treasury itself". There was, in fact, no forerunner of the Plowden five-year forecasts. From Plowden a Public Expenditure Survey first developed which was greatly improved and extended in 1969–71. A Public Expenditure Survey Committee (PESC) was established within the Treasury, followed by a Programme Analysis and Review (PAR), focusing between them on the main determinants of demand for public expenditure e.g. population growth, vehicle numbers, demand for a supply of houses, trends in crime and detection rates etc.,[2] and on a more deliberate search for options and alternatives and a look again at established practices to see whether they were still justified or should be replaced?"[3]

Increasing the data available and the analytical sophistication which is applied to that data is not, asserted Alexander, a substitute for policy decisions, but the provision of tools to enable more informed decision taking – informed about the competing needs, the competing ways of meeting them and the consequences. It is a process by which the choices facing government are posed more acutely and which therefore imposes the need for choice and the ordering of priorities more firmly on government. Decision-takings by public representatives in local government are also supported by the development of equivalent processes and techniques. Social value-judgments might have less room for manoeuvre as the imperatives of a situation are made abundantly clear to the politicians, but in the final analysis subjective considerations can play a key role in decisions, particularly those affecting social welfare issues – which in Scottish public investment terms makes up more than half of all public investment.

"It is perhaps natural to react to this assertion of supremacy of the political judgment, the hunch or the prejudice, by

2   idem, p. 47.
3   idem, p. 48.

expressing the hope that investment decisions in the public corporations are free from such influences."

Industrial enterprises whose function was the provision of goods and services for purchase, are closer to market influences and therefore to objective tests of what people wanted. But the *raison d'être* of nationalisation has been frequently the inappropriateness of market forces as a means of achieving ends judged to be socially desirable. As an example, a nationalised industry's prices differ from the prices which would obtain if the industry were free from the particular form of governmental influence which affects nationalised industries. Obviously, this weakens the approach to public sector investment decisions which takes as the datum line the rate of return on capital invested in the private sector. If in future public and private sectors continue to operate under the same system of price controls, an equivalent rate-of-return approach would have a better basis in economic logic. Even then the extent to which public sector enterprises were expected to serve social, as well as commercial, objectives had to be seen as a further reason why it was doubtful whether any clear link could be established between public and private sectors which would guide the decision makers in the efficient allocation of scarce capital between them. If the objectives differ the tests cannot be the same.

British Rail provides an illustration of the point. Investment programmes could be worked out on a cost-benefit basis, with capital costs charged in a way thought to reflect the overall scarcity of capital in the economy, thus relating to the rate of return it could earn in other (private sector) uses, (the test discount rate). If, for any reason, the out-turn is substantially different from the forecast, there could be a Ministerial view that the service should nonetheless be maintained, even that the new investment should be undertaken to that end. The result would be a larger than estimated deficit which reflected the *judgment* that a service need not meet the criteria suggested by a social cost-benefit analysis, priced commercially, to be socially worthwhile.

"Who is there who can place his hand on his or her heart and swear that he or she has not been glad to enjoy some such non-commercial benefit?" said Alexander. "Some of us may enjoy such a benefit every day as we travel to and from work."

In certain cases there was a statutory obligation, as with the electricity supply industry, to provide supplies to rural areas. In other cases, like the railways, social responsibilities might be adopted because of Ministerial suggestion. In others, the provision of employment in areas of above-average unemployment might produce non-commercial behaviour.

An American academic[4] brought this out as part of his conclusion regarding the allocation of resources to – and within – the fuel industries in Britain, and with special reference to Scotland.

" . . . coal industry profit rates have not been markedly low, the popular conception to the contrary notwithstanding. Loans have probably not been much, if at all, cheaper for public firms, all things considered, than for comparable private firms. Nor has cross subsidising been very extensive in the coal or gas industry (when it occurs at all). Moreover, the coal pits and gas plants showing losses have been tightly clustered in a few locales in high correlation with local problems of unemployment and arrested economic growth.

"Several tests were also made on the efficiency of the merging shape of output and capital in the coal and Scottish gas industries. The econometric tests suggest that the long run trends are fundamentally sound, not generally divorced from economic considerations. Most Coal Board investment has probably been as productive, in a commercial and economic sense, as investment in private industries. Allowing for additional social benefits, it might have been considerably more fruitful, compared to private industry, rather than less."[5]

Despite the claims for nationalised industry in terms of their commercial performance, Professor William G. Shepherd

4 William G. Sheperd.
5 William G. Shepherd, *Economic Performance under Public Ownership*. Yale University Press, 1965, p. 14.

came down strongly, as Alexander did, against both the practicality and the propriety of judging the nationalised industries against standards of commercial performance established in the private sector.

"Recent debate has focused narrowly on internal allocation within the public corporations and has encouraged a new commercial orientation for nationalised industry. This criterion was found, upon examination, to be largely empty and dubious as a guide for solving the really difficult allocational problems of the public corporations. If the public corporations were tiny and faced purely competitive markets, if there were no joint costing problems and if their decisions had no social impact, then a commercial orientation would not be actively inappropriate. But to say this is to show how narrow the suitability of the commercial approach is. Under other, more prevalent conditions, commercial rules will often be empty or wrong, and policy will necessarily be framed *ad hoc* for the specific situations."[6]

"So what is left?" said Alexander. If, because of their scale and the diversity of each of their range of products, together with the extent to which they must meet social as well as commercial objectives, it is inappropriate to give substantial weight to market tests in determining the investment policies of the public corporations, must the conclusion be that there is no rational basis on which such decisions can be taken? Does anything go – or not go – merely on the basis of the collective wisdom of boards and government? If such complex structures are persisted with and given conflicting objectives, the problem of stewardship cannot be resolved by the tidy formulae of test-discount rate, marginal cost-pricing and the rest. Cost-benefit ratios go some way to resolving the problem of multi-objectives, but in a dynamic situation with economic policies and social objectives sometimes having to be adjusted, while major investment programmes were being laid down, and having to be adjusted frequently over the life time of such investments, the technique did not supply a once-and-for-all answer as to

6 *idem*, p. 139.

how the balance could be struck between social and policy-oriented aims on the one hand and commercial aims on the other.

Political Judgments

The argument has already been put forward that political judgments must infuse the process of public sector investment. The emphasis is on "political" judgment as distinct from analytical calculation as a necessary component of all investment decisions, possibly more so in the private sector, where the degree of uncertainty can be much greater than in the public sector. But whereas business judgment is the attempt to apply wisdom to future commercial circumstances and the commercially-oriented behaviour of customers and competitors, political judgment is much more the attempt to strike a balance between competing interests – e.g. the locational advantages of site A over site B, which could minimise costs and prices and maximise profits, against the social policy and advantages of site B over site A, as a re-distributor of job opportunities to where they are most needed.

Politicians and civil servants cannot be expected to conjure up an acceptable replica of the public's attitude to public investment out of their own subjective consciousness. They had to function as a transfer mechanism through which public attitudes were brought to bear on such decisions. The civil servant and the politician, in the papers they wrote and the arguments they advanced in committee, play a crucial last stage in the decision-taking process, but the process leading up to this crucial stage should be informed by analysis, the posing of alternative choices open, the recognition of alternatives foregone when each choice open is selected, and all of it should be as open as possible to public probing and discussion, so that the decision takers are aware of public interests and attitudes.

Alexander thought that the proposals for a Scottish Assembly took on a special interest. The case for it is that it will enable decisions to be taken more out in the open and therefore enable, in the end, politicians to make decisions which are more responsible and to what Alexander called the "needs of the people".

The U.K. Parliament had achieved some success in monitoring the effectiveness of government in managing public expenditure, but had not got into the decision-taking process itself to any great extent. Goldman, commenting on the two-day debates on successive White Papers disclosing the government's policies and programmes for public spending wrote: "No one, however generously inclined could describe them as other than disappointing."[7] He concluded ". . . policy-making has hitherto been a jealously guarded prerogative of the executive branch, though subject to the closest scrutiny and criticism of the legislature. Successive governments have shown a willingness to share some aspects of this role with Parliament – but only some, and then of the government's own choosing. I believe myself there is sufficient scope here for useful co-operation between these two branches of our constitution to absorb the energies of both for a considerable time to come."[8]

Alexander believed that the area for "useful co-operation" could be much more effectively developed if the scale and scope of the issues to be decided were to be reduced, and more so than ever if such a process of sharing in decision-taking were to be developed at the out-set in a new assembly attracting widespread interest and support. A Scottish executive which developed such a relationship with a Scottish Assembly, both informed and armed with an array of techniques now available for investment appraisal, with published material available for discussion in the Assembly and beyond, would have an unrivalled opportunity of extending the concept of "open government", and of improving the extent to which social policies reflected public interests and attitudes.

It can be argued that such an open system would, by providing greater scope for pressure group activities, make rational decision-taking more difficult, but that brought about

7   Goldman, ibid., p. 18.
8   *idem*, p. 23.

the realisation that, in social policy with conflicting interests, no social philosopher has been able to provide either a definition of, or rules-of-thumb for, rational decisions. Democracy put a higher value on the diffusion of decision-taking and the curbing of arbitrary authority than on economic or commercial rationality, and there-ever social objectives were part of the package, democratic insistence infused decision-taking with a better reflection of the "public interest" than could the most dedicated, rationally-calculating and socially-sensitive group of executives ever in St Andrew's House.

The scope of an executive-assembly joint decision-taking process so far is not clear. The proposals for Scotland on Democracy and Devolution published as a White Paper in September, 1974[9] were provisional and imprecise: the Assembly is to have a legislative role and powers within fields in which separate Scottish legislation already exists such as housing, health and education.

In the White Paper the Government proposed the creation of a directly elected Assembly which, though having certain common characteristics and relationships to the central Government, would reflect the difference in governmental structure. The membership, function and procedure would need some detailed study and consideration but some key aspects are:

(a) membership will be on the same system as that of the U.K. Parliament – a single member elected for a geographical area: (b) the assembly will assume some of the executive functions of the Scottish Office and of nominated authorities: (c) the financial allocation will be in the form of a block grant from the U.K. Parliament under arrangements which would account for both local needs and the desirability of some uniformity of standards of services and of contributions in all parts of the U.K. It will be for the assembly to judge among competing priorities: (d) the assembly is not expected to assume existing powers from local government.

9 *Democracy and Devolution – Proposals for Scotland and Wales.* Cmnd 5732, H.M.S.O., 1974.

The U.K. Parliament and the central government ministers will remain fully responsible for the overall interests of the U.K., and Scotland will still retain the same number of Members of Parliament (71) with the Secretary of State as a full member of the Government.

The Scottish Assembly is not expected to be formed until about 1977.

The extension of the responsibilities of the Secretary of State for Scotland in the field of industry may point the way to a solution of the problem of how to maintain a general uniformity of approach in the United Kingdom as a whole to the allocation of resources, to taxation arrangements and to the overall management of the economy and to how far executive powers over trade, industry, and employment should be devolved to a Scottish Assembly, said Alexander.

The relations, if any, between the Scottish executive and assembly on the one hand, and the Secretary of State and the Development Agency responsible to him on the other, were clearly of great importance and would be difficult to establish without complicating some areas of policy-making in which one head is better than two. It might be difficult to avoid incompatible decisions in the fields of economic and physical planning if one set of decisions lay with a Secretary of State and the other with an executive-assembly. If such a division were to exist, the possibility of developing more sensitive indicators of "the public interest" through discussion of public expenditure and investment policy in an assembly would be very severely curtailed, and in some cases when it existed, would be so incomplete as to create frustrations rather than improve decision-taking.

"Shopping List" Approach

Without detailed information on the costs, and expected returns, both commercial and social, of alternative investment possibilities it is impossible (or should be) for an economist *qua* economist to choose and explain the basis of his choice of investment projects. Professional pride and propriety limited Alexander in what he had to say on investment projects.

He took as a starting point, however, the recommendations made at the International Forum in 1973 by his colleague at Strathclyde University Professor Ronald E. Nicoll.[10] Nicoll had made eleven recommendations, two of which were primarily concerned with administrative and governmental structure but all of which involved public expenditure mostly in the form of public investment. Although there were overlapping elements within the recommendations, they could be clarified as follows ("government" is taken to cover both national and local government action):

(a) *Infrastructure expenditure and investment:* Support for a new axis from south-west to north-east of Scotland, with oil exploration facilitated, and the establishment of an Environmental Protection Fund (b) *Government action aimed to encourage industrial development:* Establishment of a Development Corporation to undertake physical developments of national importance; industrial sites at Grangemouth and Hunterston to be zoned, serviced and prepared at once with similar developments in the Cromarty Firth in the 1980s. A manpower policy to provide for improved re-training programmes and better career prospects. (c) *Financial support from Government to encourage economic activity:* Encouragement for growth in agriculture, fishing, forestry and tourism with priority given to those interests outwith the principal industrial growth zone. More R and D programmes in the private sector (if necessary with Government financial assistance). (d) *Government industrial and commercial activity:* Production of 8 million tons per annum of steel in Scotland; more R and D programmes in the public sector; improved and co-ordinated transport plan covering all modes of transportation in Scotland.

Nicoll's report, *A Future for Scotland*, depended very considerably upon initiative, expenditure and investment by Government. The importance of private initiative and invest-

10   Ronald E. Nicoll, "Future for Scotland", in *Scotland's Goals* pp. 48–9. Scottish Council (Development and Industry), Collins, 1974,

ment in addition to these contributions from Government was not underestimated. Private firms responding to the opportunities which Government action made more attractive, by grants and infrastructure development, was at the heart of the policy recommended, and without such responses there would be no point in the plan and no future. In some cases the activities of private and public sectors were seen to be co-ordinated, e.g. the co-ordinated transport plan would involve not only British Rail, the Scottish Transport Group, British Airways, and the several local government transport operations, but also British Caledonian Airways, North of Scotland Shipping Company, Western Ferries and the several independent bus operations. In other cases, e.g. the encouragement of industrial complexes at Grangemouth, Hunterston and Cromarty Firth, some direct industrial activity by Government and Government agencies would almost certainly be necessary. Most of the local or regional government elements in the policies (such as housing) are strongly influenced by central government.

Alexander listed the government policies, ranging from infrastructure expenditure, roads, harbours etc., through to direct industrial investment e.g. steel to consider the possible relationships of the present Scottish Office, the future executive-Assembly structure, and the Department of Industry and the priorities which might and should be chosen.

Sir Samuel Goldman[11] (among others) had argued that the total volume of public expenditure could not be set at some arbitrary level, but could only be determined after discussion on its components. Once claims were made, a process of trimming took place, and that was affected by some view of what the aggregate could be. A view of whether it could rise or fall, and by how much, was the determining factor. That was the process when crisis cuts were the order of the day, and although there were differences between the process of constructing a total and of cutting back on one, there were also similarities. If a major increase in public investment was

11   Goldman, ibid., p. 27.

desired in a particular sector, e.g. road building and other infrastructure or steel manufacture, good administrative practice and better economics would be to at least explore what elements of public expenditure could be cut, so that the total public spending did not take all the strain.

"The first major policy issue to be decided – in my opinion – is the extent to which 'advance infrastructure provision' should be a major element in policy and therefore in investment expenditure."

It has become almost a habit of thought to argue for this approach, but in earlier history when economic growth was rapid, it was more usual for infrastructure to respond to commercial developments, than for faith to be pinned on the alternative order of things. Two explanations underlie the emphasis on "infrastructure first". The first is the growth of physical planning and environmental consciousness and a worthy determination not to make the same mistakes again as were made in earlier industrial revolutions. But the building of under-used and painfully uneconomic bridges and roads was neither a defence of the environment nor a cost-effective way of inducing growth or creating jobs (except in their building – and perhaps gathering the tolls!) The second explanation is, that infrastructure policy measures have been preferred to alternatives which brought government into more direct participation in industry, a preference which could be given a degree of mild support from economic theory, which considers that the distortions to the market mechanism and thus to allocative efficiency which would arise from government subsidy, or direct intervention in industry, are more serious than from government expenditure on "public goods" and other forms of infrastructure.

Alexander argued that it might be more productive for government to become involved directly in industry either directly or through a private-public partnership than spend money on infrastructure which might not necessarily attract industry into a particular area.

A Scottish Assembly would need to discuss objectives and

priorities and also to discuss a policy for public expenditure based on the work of a Scottish PESC and a Scottish PAR. On the assumption that they would be similar to those in *A Future for Scotland*[12] what other major objectives had to be considered? With the emphasis placed on infrastructure spending as an instrument of a policy for economic growth, what particular infrastructure investments should take priority?

After housing (in which social considerations must continue to outweigh other ones for some time to come) there could be little argument that *transport* and *communications* must be given priority. Infrastructure spending on roads, and harbours had to be considered in conjunction with public and private sector investment in airports, railways, ships and buses. Alexander considered that it had been a defect of the Toothill Report that it had underplayed the importance of transport costs as a factor deterring economic growth in Scotland, and that for too many years this had remained part of the conventional wisdom. The case for increased investment in transport – infrastructure and direct provision of services, was that distance and associated cost create problems for Scottish industry in relation both to suppliers and markets within Scotland and beyond. The Scottish Council had advocated a 100% transport subsidy, paid from the EEC Regional Development Fund to firms located in peripheral areas, for that part of costs attributable to their distance from the nearest non-peripheral area. Such an approach has many problems of definition and of creating new anomalies and thereby generating further demands for subsidising on grounds of equity. The alternative, which Alexander preferred, is to put all the emphasis, and the available funds, into improved communications, thus reducing the disadvantages which exist. Better communications did, however, open an area up to competition as well as opening out opportunities for those located within it, which is one reason why, on economic grounds, the improvement of communications is preferable to direct subsidy.

Within total expenditure on improving communications,

12 A "Future for Scotland", ibid., p. 130.

more consideration had to be given to defining objectives and determining the most cost effective ways of meeting these, e.g. a decision-taking process must be created within which a choice between rail and road for freight can be taken.

Alexander listed some of the items on his "shopping list" – priorities which he considered needed examining.

(a) The importance of freight movement by rail because of the character of industrial developments, and because it would improve the environment and reduce congestion. (b) The electrification of rail lines north of Glasgow to Inverness and Invergordon (on the Cromarty Firth). (c) Integration of airport developments into an overall plan for transport. (Developments at Edinburgh Airport are the responsibility of the British Airports Authority, which is responsible to one Government Minister and is having 75% of the cost of development financed by the Department of Trade, and consults with the Scottish Office about plans. One of the proposals for devolution is that "within the British Airports Authority a separate organisation to be known as Scottish Airports is to be set up".[13] Such a structure would have clearly unresolved problems of harmonisation and it is not obvious how a Scottish executive-assembly, armed with its own Public Expenditure Survey, could play an effective role in determining priorities.

There has been a long period of uncertainty and concern in Scotland about the future of Prestwick, and the four-fold increase in the cost of aviation fuel in recent months cannot have strengthened the position there. Nevertheless, the case for consolidating and developing this international airport is strong and it is encouraging to note that BAA plans general airport developments there over the next five years, to cost £4 million at March 1974 prices. If the decision-making process were more closely related to Scottish policy-making, it is likely that such a development would be expanded and perhaps brought forward. A possible administrative framework which would maintain the necessary close liaison with airport planning

---

13 *Democracy and Devolution,* ibid., p. 10; e.g. Tom Johnston, Hugh Ogilvy and others.

in other parts of the U.K. would be a parallel with the relationship between the Forth and Clyde Ports Authorities who get help and guidance from the National Ports Council, but retain authority in Scotland. The Forth Ports Authority is engaged in an investment programme which will come close to doubling the present capital employed by it, relating to the complex development at Grangemouth and also to oil development. One consequence of such decisions being taken under a Scottish umbrella could be that more emphasis is placed on rationalising port developments within Scotland, placing less emphasis on competition between Scottish ports and more on holding and attracting business which otherwise goes through other U.K. ports.) (d) The supply of fuel and power, vital to any plan for economic development. The difficulty of arriving at the best investment decisions is illustrated by the influence which the high price of coal had until Autumn 1974 (when oil prices were raised). Studies by the electricity boards showed returns of 50% per annum and more on capital spent on converting coal-fired to oil-fired stations, and on the basis of four power stations, representing 10% of the South of Scotland Electricity Board's total capacity, having been converted or partially converted to oil. The reduction of grit-emission was a social benefit, but the costs are now greatly in excess of those used in the calculations which led to the decision to convert. Reorganising the administrative structure of decision-taking could not be expected to avoid uncertainties and turn-abouts of that kind. It was not surprising that both Boards – the South and the North of Scotland Hydro Electric Board – placed greater emphasis on the need for flexibility in the choice of fuels.

One development of particular interest and promise could be the use of that part of North Sea natural gas which is unsuitable for the national gas grid, for the generation of electricity in East Coast power stations. The goal of (relatively) cheap power as a prime mover in Scottish industrial development was now more realistic than when it was first advanced and would certainly require the attention in any future Public Expenditure Survey for Scotland.

Alexander argued, too, that it is important to develop research for alternative fuels within the energy policy. The EEC is in the process of formulating an energy policy which includes the idea of increasing by a factor of ten, over the next ten years, the contribution of nuclear power to the total power situation. (*Britain's nuclear programme is included in that tenfold increase. The nuclear industry in Britain has been moribund for the past five years but a small programme of 4,000 megawatts initially is being started, and within three years the programme will have accelerated. A large amount of nuclear power is in service at present and the amount of nuclear power in Scotland per capita is high. Britain generates more electricity from nuclear power than any other European country*). A massive research programme for the development of hydrogen as a major energy carrier has been advocated by Professor Nicoll,[14] and although it is a long-term project, no progress even of an exploratory nature has been made in the last twelve months.

Shopping lists unrelated to price-tags and an expenditure constraint could be infinitely expanded, admitted Alexander, but the economist's role was not to encourage such fantasy. Without detailed and up-to-date financial information there was no possibility of coming down rationally, far less unequivocally, in favour of particular projects.

Detailed information about projects is necessary in the future to provide open discussion. It would be the only possible basis on which the Scottish public could accept that on some issues the efficiency of the U.K. economy would be enhanced by decisions which cut across Scottish aspirations. Without the facts and informed discussion there would be a tendency, regrettable perhaps but inevitable, to believe that Scottish interests were being overlooked and it would become more and more difficult to secure the necessary harmonisation of major investment decisions within the U.K. in the interests of everyone.

Scotland's devolutionary future will require much more open decision-taking if it is to advance rather than retard the rational use of public resources, measured against the public's own estimate of its interest.

14 "Future for Scotland", in *Scotland's Goals*, ibid.

According to the Scottish Council Research Institute in 1972/3 public expenditure represented 42·5% of the United Kingdom's Gross Domestic Product. In the same year public expenditure in Scotland (including defence, foreign affairs and National Debt interest pro-rated on a population basis) was 52% of Scottish GDP. SCRI then added in current expenditure of nationalised industries and suggested that expenditure might be 60% or more of Scottish GDP. (Alexander considers this high – and that his own figure might be on the low side. He suggests the figure is somewhere between 33⅓ and 60%.)

Table 1 Public expenditure in Scotland and Great Britain, 1972/3

	Scotland £m	G.B. £m	Scotland % G.B.
Agriculture, forestry, fishing	93·3	438	21·3
Trade, industry and employment:			
Regional policy	84·0	245	34·3
Other assistance to industry, and employment services	108·3	940	11·5
Nationalised industries' capital expenditure	202·5	1,683	12·0
Transport	130·1	1,251	10·3
Housing	259·4	1,446	17·9
Education	423·3	3,798	11·1
Health and personal social services	331·7	3,069	10·8
Environmental services	132·4	1,444	9·2
Social Security	508·6	5,005	10·2
Miscellaneous:			
Research councils	10·4	140	7·4
Law and order	74·2	878	8·5
Arts	3·3	44	7·5
Common services	65·3	859	7·6
total	2,426·8	21,240	11·4

Sources: Scottish Abstract of Statistics, H.M.S.O., 1974.
National Income and Expenditure, H.M.S.O., 1973.

Note: The figure for research councils does not include £4·8 million of grants and grants in aid made by the Department of Agriculture and Fisheries to research institutes.

chapter 6

Private Investment

The views put forward by Professor Alexander on public sector investment received support, in part, from the Scottish general manager of one nationalised industry, and criticism from the chairman of another.

And Gerald Elliot who spoke on private sector investment, put on another hat – as chairman of the Forth Ports Authority – to join the criticism.

Agreement, on the matter of investment in transport, came from a transport man, David Cobbett, general manager of the Scottish Region of British Rail. Such investment he asserted should be high on the priority list because –

It led to competitiveness in markets, cost effectiveness in production, energy conservation if the right form (of transport) was chosen, environmental protection, in that it allowed industrial activity to be dispersed, assisted mobility of manpower and mobility of activity, and spread the benefits of those activities to areas not immediately related to oil or other forms of work. More onshore investment which the oil industry required had to go into transport in all forms, whatever it might be called – roads, track, runways, or oil pipelines, and vehicles and rolling stock. And choices had to be made. Perhaps, quite naturally, he thought that in some cases rail provided a greater cost-effectiveness and cited the amount of money being spent on doubling the capacity of the A9 road, from Perth to Inverness, totalling £120 million, which was twelve times the amount needed to achieve a similar capacity on a parallel railway. The example was not a condemnation, because each form of transport had its proper place and had to be sustained. What concerned Cobbett was the lack of total investment in transport in Scotland, not only over the last few years but also for the relatively poor appreciation of the need in the years ahead.

"It is vital that all opinions in Scotland and the United Kingdom, be it political, industrial, economic or just public opinion, identifies the need for a greatly improved transport system, and the urgent need to invest in it," he said. "Transport for Scotland and oil must be seen as an extra to any overall U.K. requirement."

Disagreement with Alexander's views on the nationalised industries, however, came from Frank Tombs, chairman of the South of Scotland Electricity Board. It was, in his view, dangerous to propound the theory that commercial criteria should not be applied to an essentially growth industry like electricity. The industry had been nationalised, not to create an institution to serve what was regarded as a social need, but to put 625 utilities together in a much smaller number and make available very big economies of scale. There was no reason why the industry should not continue to trade on a basically commercial basis. It was not only desirable, but essential, for the nation's benefit.

And Elliot disputed the view of the possible relationship of nationalised industries and an elected Assembly. He did not consider that the boards of nationalised industries would want investment plans made centrally, adapted and decided by an elected body.

"Most boards would like nationalised industries to be free to work according to normal commercial criteria except in very special cases," he asserted. "I think the justification is that the more political involvement there is, the less likely those industries are to do their main job properly which is to provide goods and services at a cheap and competitive rate."

But what about private sector investment in Scotland and the U.K.? Elliot, vice chairman and managing director of Christian Salvesen Ltd. a company well known for whaling, and now in shipping, fishing and the oil industry, said that it has been low for many years, along with growth – and has caused much concern to successive governments.

The level of private investment in the U.K. is governed by somewhat different factors than public investment, though he suspected not all that different. But it is more sensitive to profit margins, taxations, special incentives, and a general feeling of business confidence, than public enterprises which worked, as such supporting industries are able to do, on longer term plans.

The causes of the low investment in growth, as with many economic problems, are complex, with their roots deeply buried in the history of the society of the country. There is a clear correlation in developed countries between high investment and high growth e.g. Japan, the outstanding growth economy, invested 31.3% of its income from 1967–71 against the U.K. 15.9%. In addition the U.K. investment has not only been lower but less productive than in other countries.

Countries with the lowest investment in recent years, U.K. and the United States, are those with the most developed capital markets and stock exchanges. In high-growth economies, Japan and Germany, the banks play a large part in the long-term financing of industry. It is quite possible that the very efficiency and transparency of the capital market in Britain may have been unconducive to high investment. Companies who rely principally on equity finance, have had to show high returns on capital and pay high dividends to satisfy shareholders and keep their market ratings. Less cash has been kept for investment, and long-maturing investments, which might temporarily reduce returns on capital, have been avoided. In contrast, in countries where capital is raised more through the banks than from the public through stock exchanges, companies set themselves lower targets for returns on capital, being content with little more than what was required to service and pay back their loans; cash was ploughed back instead of being distributed as dividend; and further bank loans were available to back expansion. Norway is an extraordinary example, on a small scale, of this pattern. Most of the quoted companies are shipping companies, which plough back their earnings, give virtually nothing to their shareholders (except a good dinner once a year), and yet maintain respectable stock exchange ratings on the basis of their growth in earnings and assets.

Elliot was not recommending, even if there was some truth in the thesis, that Britain should try to model the private sector according to that pattern. In Britain there is a movement in this direction. Financing of industry by banks and other institutions has increased in recent years, and with the collapse of the stock exchange is likely in the near future to be the only way of raising new funds for investment. But a private sector working on low returns and high loans is loaded with risk. If it is in a prosperous economy, with gentle inflation and low rates of interest, then it is a magic recipe for success. Some countries have had these conditions continuously for the past twenty years. But times ahead will be much sterner. A whiff of recession, and a slump in world trade, could leave many such companies in the hands of unwilling banks and make the conservative financing of U.S. and U.K. companies look a virtue. Apart from this, the low-return formula will only work to the extent that industry has the operational efficiency to make its investments work as planned. This quality has been lacking in the British economy. Companies must limit their investments to those offering high returns, because they are not confident that the equipment they order will arrive in time, will work when it does arrive, and can be efficiently and economically manned when it starts working. Until Britain can improve its performance, it could not expect to become a low return, high investment, economy.

Elliot thought that the last government had been groping towards a low-return investment formula as the means of increasing investment in the U.K. However, in his view, it had ducked the problems of operational efficiency (too difficult for any government to face) and the consequences of failure. It seemed to be pressing for more investment even if the best commercial judgment decided it would not pay. No doubt the state would be ready to pay the bill for the bad investments, as it does so readily in the public sector, but it would be a considerable waste of the country's resources.

The field where governments can act effectively to encourage investment is taxation. The provision of free depreciation to most new investment, which had been introduced a few years ago, was an incentive of enormous value. It met completely the long-standing grievance of industry, which pointed out that until it had earned back the cost of its investment it had not made a profit and should not pay tax. The one drawback was that it favoured the "haves" against the "have-nots". The firms who had other profits to put against the free depreciation of the new assets got a big advantage. Companies starting from scratch got relief on the profits which they earned, but nothing like the same benefits as established companies. Against this, the general tax system had, since 1965, been progressively modified to charge money retained in the company more heavily than cash paid out in dividends. The changes were initiated in 1965 to bring the U.K. more into line with the EEC systems, where the current dogma was that earnings of a company should be returned to its shareholders, who would then be free to decide where to reinvest it. High taxation on dividends in the shareholders' hands had made nonsense of the theory, which had never been a very convincing one, and the system left was one which penalised companies if they kept and ploughed back their earnings, as they ought to do. If retention of earnings was helped fiscally, then it would encourage investment and perhaps over time focus stock exchange values more healthily on earnings rather than dividends.

Within the U.K. Scotland was a small region, affected by the same influences as the rest of the economy. Like other regions, it was handicapped by its distance from the rich markets of the south and by the centralising pull of London, but unlike some of them it had a strong, although partly obsolete, industrial background. Its investment as a percentage of income seems to have been about the same as the U.K., while income per head, starting from a lower base than the U.K. as a whole, had in recent years grown somewhat faster, reducing the percentage gap between the Scottish and U.K. income.

What guidance could then be given for private investment in the future? Two initial assumptions were made by Elliot with which not everybody might agree. The first was that regional incentives were not going to be an important factor in future to boost investment in Scotland. They were clearly important in certain fields, particularly when one wanted to establish a large new industry in the country, which could be equally attracted elsewhere. But, for most Scottish industry, he did not believe that these incentives made much difference to investment decision. They were far less important than the prospects of the industry concerned and the general prosperity of the economy. In his own company, which had carried out big investments in Scotland and England in recent years, there had not been any occasion on which the level of grants was the deciding factor.

The second assumption was that in Scotland it was necessary to continue to have an open economy. There had been much criticism recently of so-called multi-national corporations who were accused in particular of diverting capital abroad to produce in low-wage areas in competition with the home produce, and, more generally, of tax evasion, foreign exchange speculation and neo-colonialism. If Scotland became a closed economy, then it would not only be the victim of numerous English multi-nationals, but a nation of exploiting multi-nationals itself. There was hardly a large company in Scotland which did not have more operations outside of Scotland than in it. Elliot believed that the activities of multi-nationals were largely beneficent whether on a U.K., European community, or world scale, and that it would be better to break barriers down than to erect them. Scotland should welcome investment from outside and embrace the opportunities of growth through investments, in England and abroad, of Scottish companies. To put restrictions on England or U.S. investment in Scotland as has been suggested by some economic nationalists, would provoke a devastating backlash which would ravage many Scottish companies whose strength lies in their operations outside of the country. Exports, which allowed Scottish companies to operate world-wide while remaining securely based at home, were only part of the answer. Some companies, e.g. in building or service industries, could only expand by investment outside Scotland, others had to build factories abroad to meet requirements of the countries concerned. In any case, as a small country, the Scots could not afford to be nationally restrictive. Norway would, apart from the oil prospect, be a very poor place if her shipping companies had not invested very substantially to give her a leading place in international shipping and contribute large overseas earnings to her balance of payments.

It might seem a cliché to suggest that the Scots should select the industries which they are good at and concentrate on investing in them. At any one time the options for good investment for the individual company were limited. Any manager would do all he could to find opportunities in his own industry, which he knew thoroughly, rather than launch out into uncharted seas. Some companies were forced to do this anyway, and it could be a painful business. His own company, when the Antarctic whaling industry declined, had to turn to completely different fields, and it made plenty of mistakes in the process. Companies were well advised to stick to their own trade if they still saw a good future growth in it. But the Scots had perhaps been too loyal to industries which were inevitably declining, and not flexible enough in looking for industries which would use part of the skills they had in new and promising markets.

Private industry in Scotland is sufficiently, but not too, enterprising. We would be likely to find opportunities in the industries at which they are good at, or potentially good at, engineering and shipbuilding, some textiles, fishing and food-processing and electronics. Then there was oil. People from the West of Scotland might not agree but he believed that with the already broadly based industry and the advent of oil, the Scots no longer needed to look for entirely new industries to strengthen the Scottish economy as successive governments had in the 1950s and 1960s. There was enough to build on, and this would be supplemented by the new industries which started up, unplanned, in any thriving economy.

Oil was a particularly suitable industry to arrive on Scotland's doorstep. Shipbuilding, engineering and electronics were all important elements in the offshore industry, and Scotland had them. The strength in fishing gave an excellent background for the running of supply boats and other support ships, and there were under-used ports to serve them.

"What we must now do is to adapt our skills and investment so that we can in time do the job better than our American friends and become the centre of an international and, I hope, multi-national industry, repeating what they achieved in the Gulf of Mexico fifteen years ago." he said. The U.K. has been slow off the mark in some areas. The offshore drilling industry had been built up in the United States by independent contractors with no ties with the oil companies. With the opening up of the North Sea a number of European countries had entered the business – Norwegian, French, Italian and British. The drilling unit is the spearhead of the offshore oil industry – from it flow the main requirements for supplies, boat services, machinery and skills. Yet U.K., which has by far the largest share of the North Sea oil areas, had no more than six rigs on order out of a world total of about 150 units. The Norwegian commitment was a striking comparison – over 50 units.

The Norwegian shipowners have, as on other occasions, let their enthusiasm carry them away without proper consideration of how they would be employed and where they would find the experts to man their rigs. But even so, the response of British industry to the opportunity is disappointing. The only consolation is that nearly half the U.K. contribution is from Scotland.

Scotland seems to be doing better in other sectors of the oil industry. There is no lack of companies and individuals ready to take up the shore-based service industries which are an important part of the oil business. Engineering companies would probably find that for the really specialised products, such as drill bits and blow-out preventers, the market is dominated by U.S. companies with world reputations and that it would be foolish to compete. But there are many other less special machinery items which could be added satisfactorily to existing lines. The first drillship for Salvesen had 100% U.S. equipment, but No. 2 would have 40% British equipment, most of it cheaper than its U.S. counterpart.

The real drag on Scotland's involvement in offshore oil is not the lack of capital, and still less the lack of initiative. It is the lack of expertise. The skills in offshore drilling and its services at present lay in the hands of a few thousand people, mainly Americans, and they were a closed community – everyone knew everyone else. The Scots, and the British had to break into this charmed circle.

It might be possible to bring some of the individuals from America into companies in Britain and learn to work with them. They then could train Scots as early as possible for the key posts, passing on to them all the skill, enthusiasm and dedication to the job. At the same time, it was necessary to ensure that the Americans who were brought in were given the same security and prospects as their Scots colleagues. The time required to develop expertise would of course vary. It would depend on the complication of each job and the experience as distinct from technical know-how which was needed to back it.

Experts were needed and the Scots require to be taught by them. But the Scots should not allow themselves to be over-impressed. There was always a tendency to exaggerate the skills needed in a particular job, and oil experts were no exception to this. The experience of newcomers has suggested that people with the appropriate background can be trained to oil jobs reasonably quickly.

It is important that investment is provided to build up the

management to look after the oil industry. Elliot considered that some Norwegian companies had made a mistake. They had shown great initiative in ordering semi-submersible rigs at an early stage, but they had signed away management rights as well as a large chunk of potential profits to established American operators. It was a safe move, but not the way to acquire oil expertise or to obtain the maximum long-term benefit. If Scottish companies brought in American partners, as they had to do, they had to beware of paying too high a price for corporate know-how or of getting themselves into a subordinate position. They might be wiser to hire individual expertise than to enter a joint venture with a company.

The government was right to exercise gentle pressure on oil companies and other oil customers to give some preference to British industry in ordering equipment and supplies to help the U.K. industry to grow through its "baby stage". It might also be advisable to require that U.S. and Norwegian rigs, which work permanently in the U.K. zone, should register in the U.K., and be manned and managed from there. Otherwise, it might be very difficult to build up on-shore industry. But no discrimination would help if the Scots could not help themselves. This meant a high level of productivity in management and staff, maximum flexibility in jobs, streamlined training and apprenticeships, and a determination in government and industry to do things better than anyone else.

It is clear that the advent of oil, combined with the continuing need to steer away from a declining industry, is going to make Scotland a swiftly changing economy in the next ten years. The change would be the responsibility of the private sector in the form of investments in new industries and products, though preferably in areas where there are already cognate skills. The innovations are going to come from private rather than public investment. Public corporations are mainly in the service and raw material sectors, and they produce for markets already provided by private enterprise. Power stations are not built speculatively, but to provide for a need which, for the economy as a whole, could be fairly accurately predicted. Even public enterprises which overlap into what were normally private enterprise areas, such as road transport, tend to be more cautious than their private sector counterparts. Parliament watches its money, and the chances of profits are less important than the possibilities of loss. So innovation is mainly left to private industry. This involved risk.

Risk is the essence of private enterprise and its main justification. It looms large in all the calculations of boards and managers when they are looking at new ventures. But, by those outside industry, its importance seems to be largely ignored. This was perhaps because the stereotype picture is of huge corporations with captive markets turning investment handles and getting a guaranteed return. Even for the largest corporations every new investment involves risk, though, to the extent that they have large assured cushions of profits, losses from ventures that go wrong need not be very painful. For medium and smaller companies, which still made up over half the productive capacity of the country, risk governs their lives whether in new markets, new products, or new industries.

It is vital that Scotland, which is trying to steer its economy into new paths, should have plenty of companies ready to take risks, whether it would be in building an oil platform or just opening a ship chandlery store. There is a widespread belief that British business people are a cautious and timid race, sluggish in responding to the golden opportunities continually dangled before them, and not to be moved even by lavish government subsidies.

Elliot's view was that the reverse was true. Industrial managers tended to be too enthusiastic, to have too many new ideas, and to be too sanguine in assessing the risks. The history of his own company over the past 100 years had illustrated this on repeated occasions.

"We should be grateful that this is so, for otherwise economic progress would come to a halt."

Keynes had something to say on it: –

"It is a characteristic of human nature that a large proportion of our positive activities depend on spontaneous optimism rather than on a mathematical expectation, whether moral or hedonistic or economic. Most, probably, of our decisions to do something positive, the full consequences of which will be drawn out over many days to come, can only be taken as a result of animal spirits – of a spontaneous urge to action rather than inaction, and not as the outcome of a weighted average of quantitative benefits multiplied by quantitative probabilities. Enterprise only pretends to itself to be mainly actuated by the statements in its own prospectus, however candid and sincere. Only a little more than an expedition to the South Pole, is it based on an exact calculation of benefits to come. Thus if the animal spirits are dimmed and the spontaneous optimism falters, leaving us to depend on nothing but a mathematical expectation enterprise will fade and die; though fears of loss may have a basis no more reasonable than hopes of profit had before."

Elliot said that British industry had seemed very unenterprising compared with the Norwegians in the oil drilling industry. However, Norwegian shipping, the dominant industry in the country, had traditionally an almost gambling attitude to investment. Being a tightknit community, the Norwegians also all tended to have the same impulse at the same time. In recent years inflation and war had made their gambles highly successful, but there had been earlier periods when blood had flowed, and it would no doubt do so again. What is required is to foster an attitude in Scotland of continual interest in new ventures, backed by a solid appreciation of what could be done and what could not be done.

If risk-taking was an essential element in economic progress, and particularly important to Scotland's changing scene, it is necessary to ensure that the government framework within which industry operated allows and encourages risk investment to take place. At present the rate of interest which capital can earn, lent without risk to government institutions, was about 15%. This is a high rate, virtually set by the government in relation to the decreasing value of money and competitive pressures from abroad. In broad terms, every industrial manager has to earn at least this return on the capital entrusted to him, otherwise he was failing in his duty to those who had entrusted their capital to him, whether they were the government, insurance companies, trade union pension funds, or private persons. When he enters risk ventures, he has to look for a return which is a good deal higher than this. The profits on the winners had to be enough to offset the losses on the fiascos, and the overall result had to turn out better than the basic 15%, otherwise there was no inducement to the shareholder to put his capital at risk at all.

There is a real danger that British governments would increasingly choose to ignore these simple truths. Beset by pressures from all sections of the community who believed that they had a right to a higher standard of living each year, regardless of whether the community had the resources to supply this, governments squeeze the earnings of industry through taxation and price control, hoping that this would get them through their short-term problems. They were fortified in this policy by the general public feeling that whereas it is entirely right for local councils to levy rates in order to pay interest on a 15% loan to build new schools, it is immoral that the same rate of return should be earned in operating an oil company or building a ship. Such short-term expedients might be necessary to meet particular crises, but in the U.K. economy they are all too readily adopted as national institutions. If this happens and governments try to get industry on the cheap, the long-term outlook would be disastrous. The future growth on which so many post-dated cheques are already being drawn would just not take place, and all the problems in Scotland and England would be multiplied.

Apart from the smothering effect of government fiscal and price control policies, the main inhibition of risk-taking is political uncertainty. Risk ventures involve so much uncertainty in themselves that if they are compounded with uncertainty on the course of the economy, or in government policy for control of the industry concerned, they might have to be abandoned. The stop-go cycles of recent years, and the prospect of their continuation, has already restrained risk investments, though it would be unfair to blame governments for conditions which were largely beyond their power to control. Broad industrial control policies, such as nationalisation, appeal to a section of the electorate, sometimes to a majority, but, whether announced or executed, they involve a severe penalty on economic progress as risk ventures are postponed or cancelled.

There is also a large part of industry in Scotland and England which is earning less than the current risk-free interest rate. Economic progress requires that companies operating below the line adjust or change their activities so that they get on the right side. The process of change involved, together with the taking of financial risk, a responsiveness in management and staff which so far had been lacking in the U.K. Particularly in Scotland, where change is required and opportunities were present, there should be much less concern in preserving old-established jobs in low return industries than getting people moved over into the high-return sectors.

"We live in a society which, despite its imperfections, provides economic growth by free movement of its resources to meet changing demands. If we want economic growth, or even economic stability, we must not hamper this process."

During a period of fast industrial development in a new area, such as oil, all sorts of discomforts and untidinesses arise. Manpower shortages occur, new-comers have to be put into makeshift housing, local authority services are stretched, earnings shoot up and embarrass traditional industries. Such upsets were the price of economic growth and, rather than resist them, the use of social organisations to make them as painless as possible should take place.

A healthy private sector with a high investment rate was vital to Scotland's economic progress. The opportunities were there, particularly in the oil industry and everyone had to do their part to grasp them.

And just how willing are people to grasp the opportunities?

Stuart Black, chairman of the large, Scottish-based General Accident Fire and Life Assurance Corporation complained that, when the Labour Party gained power in February 1974, Prime Minister Harold Wilson had stated that he was determined that private enterprise should know where it stood in relation to the private sector. Private enterprise had yet to find out. Black was critical of government which had interfered and made threats for a long time. The Conservative government had been afraid of money running away, of bold expansion, overheating and other troubles – and had "clobbered" the property sector. Uncertainty had been created, the capital market had started going down hill and had dried up. The Labour government was threatening nationalisation in another way – *participation*. Black had quarrelled with participation in some forms. If money is being given to industry, the government has a responsibility to see that the money is being used properly. In the insurance industry, as with investment trusts and bankers, they have to do with the money what is right for the shareholders, and in the case of insurance, for policy holders and the pension funds.

Black claimed that it was not possible to invest in industry because the problems were not clear. There was a lack of stability and confidence. His firm was a service company, and a multi-national company involved in extremely vital invisible exports. He agreed with Elliot that British multi-national companies in the vast majority were beneficial to the economy.

He warned, however, that the government should not take steps in North Sea oil or elsewhere that might discourage not only British, but foreign companies investing in Scotland, and at the same time bring about a situation overseas which would stop British companies earning the large amount of foreign exchange that they already earned. His plea was for the government to allow investors to operate freely.

But even in making that plea it still appeared that there would be a hesitancy in investing. Black, himself, illustrated a point – perhaps unconsciously – by stating that in the Autumn of 1973 former Prime Minister Edward Heath had scolded the insurance business at a luncheon for not investing in industry when he (Heath) had created a climate and they were not responding.

"Well, suppose we had, we would have lost half our money or very near it by now", said Black.

The scolding was repeated at the International Forum in the Autumn of 1974. It was delivered by Bruce Millan over Black's allegation that the government's plans *vis-à-vis* private enterprise and nationalisation were vague and that there should be less interference.

"It is really rather unrealistic to expect government of whatever political complexion to leave industry alone, and not to be very concerned and intervene quite actively in many matters which concern the private industry.

"The real complaint of industry is not that governments intervene, but that sometimes they intervene in ways that industry finds unacceptable".

And it is not true that the Labour government was vague about its intentions about nationalisation. It has been all laid out in a White Paper and although industrialists might actively disagree with what the government intended doing, in relation to private industry, it could not accuse the government of not being explicit.

In the White Paper *The Regeneration of British Industry* the Government outlined the proposals for the setting up of two systems, *Planning Agreements* with major firms in key sectors of industry, and a *National Enterprise Board* to provide the means for direct public initiatives in particular key sectors of industry. The argument for doing so was that Britain as a whole in the last thirty years had not been able, for a variety of reasons – social, economic and industrial – to fully harness the resources of skill and ability which it should have been able to command.

Compared to the country's competitors there had been a steady falling behind, and an inability to find the self-confidence to bridge the gap. As the gap widened, the investment and new industrial relationships required to maintain living standards had become progressively more difficult to secure. In 1971, investment for each worker in British manufacturing industry was less than half that in France, Japan or the United States, and well below that in Germany or Italy. In spite of the measures taken since then to encourage investment, it had still lagged behind, and was significantly less in 1972 and 1973 than in 1970. Britain was also less effective than its competitors in making effective use of manufacturing equipment. With the lack of demand for investment in manufacturing industry, funds that could have been used to improve and modernise British industry had been deployed elsewhere – in the last ten years the rate of direct investment by British firms overseas had more than trebled.

Successive governments had striven to correct the deficiences, both through general economic measures and by various forms of assistance to industry. But the attitudes of governments to industry, and of industry to governments had been too remote, too coloured by the concept that the Government's main function towards industry was one of regulation, to prevent the activities of industry, or the abuse of its powers, damaging the interests of other sectors of the community. The new concept is that of industry and the Government being partners in the pursuit of the objectives which spell success for industry and prosperity for Britain – and that required a closer, clearer and more positive relationship between Government and industry.

Planning Agreements The main theme of the system is a series of consultations between the Government and companies leading to an agreement about plans for the following three years which will be reviewed and "rolled forward" annually. The arrangement will be with major and strategic firms in key sectors of the manufacturing industry, and in selected industries in other sectors of particular importance to the economy. Multi-national companies will be included only in respect of their British holdings. During the transitional period the Planning Agreements will take place in those areas of particular importance and with firms involved in the export effort. In the course of the consultations, the Government will assess with the Company its needs for assistance to support and reinforce agreed company plans, with special reference to selective assistance for new employment projects in the regions. Though the principal application of the Planning Agreements will be to large companies, the Government intends in times of economic difficulty to cater for the special needs of the small businessman.

The Government is only going to be concerned with strategic issues and recognition is given that the new arrangements should not restrict the freedom of companies to respond to market changes, particularly in the export field. It is intended that there will be a greater degree of consultation with the employees through their union representatives, and companies will have to disclose a great deal more information than happens at present.

National Enterprise Board The new agency is being set up to secure where necessary large-scale sustained investment to offset the effects of the short-term pull of market forces, and one of the functions will be to build on and enlarge the activities of the former Industrial Reorganisation Corporation.

In addition, NEB will be an industrial holding company with subsidiary companies in manufacturing industry, with a number of existing Government shareholdings in companies transferred to it immediately on it being established – Rolls-Royce (1971) Ltd; International Computers (Holdings) Ltd; George Kent Ltd; Nuclear Enterprises Ltd; Dunford and Elliott Ltd; Kearney and Trecker Marwin Ltd; Norton Villiers Triumph Ltd. But holdings in shipbuilding companies or in firms whose activities are largely overseas like the British Petroleum Co. Ltd, Cable and Wireless Ltd, and the Suez Finance Company are not regarded as appropriate to be included in the new agency.

Funds of £2000 million are being made available (subject to Government and Parliamentary control) to allow the Board to –

be a new source of investment capital for manufacturing industry to supplement, not displace, the supply of investment from existing financial institutions and from companies' own resources: but in providing capital it will normally take a corresponding share in equity capital; have an entrepreneurial role in promoting industrial efficiency and profitability by promoting or assisting the reorganisation or development of an industry; have power to start new ventures and participate in joint ventures with companies in the private sector; act as an instrument through which the Government will operate directly to create employment in areas of high unemployment; give advice to Government departments, nationalised industries and private firms on financial and managerial issues; be the instrument by which the Government can extend public ownership; acquire through agreement 100% or part-holding of companies which are profitable, though at the same time take over ailing companies in danger of collapse which are required for reasons of regional employment or industrial policy.

The Scottish Development Agency, which would be responsible to the Secretary of State for Scotland, would be given a substantial measure of responsibility for the promotion of industrial and economic development. The appropriate NEB functions would be carried out in Scotland by the Scottish Development Agency. (see Chapter 9 Industry and the Community).

Another Salvesen man, chairman Harper Gow, was not impressed with the idea of the National Enterprises Board. He hoped that the banks and other financial experts would find the right way to bridge over the difficult economic period. He considered that if Scotland is going to have a thoroughly sound industry upon which future investment could be based, it is necessary that over the next year or two that industry should be sound. In the past two years the three-day week, the extraordinary rise in the costs of raw materials, and the incredible rise in rates had created the most unique situation in thirty years. Added to this was the fairly tight financial position of lending by the banks. It was vital for the future that the parts of Scottish industry which are potentially healthy, but might be going through temporary difficulties, were retained.

"I hope this could be done more through private consultations and co-operation between industry and the financial sections of the Scottish scene, rather than through Government intervention and capital gains and loans," said Gow.

He emphasised that he was not advocating a policy of keeping "lame ducks" going – but many firms merely needed under-standing and assistance to get over present problems. He considered that there is a great deal of mis-understanding between the banks and the small and medium-sized companies. Scottish industry has to learn to approach banks at an early stage of appraisal of their financial needs, to allow the planning of assistance by the banks.

The Scottish unit of the Stock Exchange in Glasgow has an efficient fund raising machinery but as the chairman William Quaile admitted, potential borrowers found the terms un-acceptable. A strong market would make fund raising easier, but a number of technical factors which are under Government control inhibit the market – Capital Gains Tax; Stamp Duty which has been doubled and is now 2% on any change in an individual's investment; the dollar premium surrender which restrains the proper management of American portfolios, and the repatriation of monies to Britain when investment trusts decided either on financial or social grounds to invest in Britain e.g. North Sea oil.

Elliot himself was critical of the taxation system. The most effective way for the Government to encourage investment is through taxation reform, he claimed. The Government has to look more seriously, with industry, at the whole taxation system, particularly in relation to inflation. He was sceptical about investment grants which are a fairly minor weapon in attracting investment to Scotland, and about Peter Jay's idea which he suggested was a type of shadow devaluation. Both remedies rested on the belief that Scotland is a static economy, doomed to grind along on relatively inefficient traditional industries requiring subsidies in one way or another to make them competitive with the rest of the U.K. But he believed that Scotland could be a dynamic economy with competitive costs more favourable than the rest of the U.K. – providing attractions for investment without the application of widespread subsidies.

chapter 7

Investment in Research

Scotland might benefit from North Sea oil to a greater or lesser extent, depending on whether one took the Government view or the Odell theory. And the expected revenue in the 1980s might pay off some of Britain's loans incurred in the 1970s and change the balance of payments situation.

But none of it would take place, according to Professor Robert Smith, former Principal and Vice Chancellor of the Heriot-Watt University at Edinburgh, unless there was a much larger investment in research immediately – and a continued investment if long term benefits were to take place.

At the same time, he warned that it would be an economic disaster if a "get rich quick" attitude was adopted, with nothing saved from the oil and gas resources to provide for the more distant future.

The immediate problem to be faced, however, was the investment needed to overcome the difficulties being encountered in the exploration and exploitation of the North Sea.

"If a very large amount of money and brainpower is not invested in new engineering and technological development then a very large quantity of oil will still be sitting beneath the waves. The problems facing the industry in getting the oil and gas are already serious."

Among some of the problems which had to be solved were the inspection of the sea-bed by navigable submersibles, rig stability, development of rigs and platform structures for use in extremely rough seas, and pipe-laying to transport the oil in great depths of water. On the materials side more effort was needed to develop corrosion-resistant materials.

A start has already been made in providing a focus for research into the problems. Heriot-Watt has an Institute of Offshore Engineering, and two Chairs, one in Offshore Engineering and the other in Petroleum Engineering, while Aberdeen University is involved in developing work on exploration for oil and gas. But the amount being spent on such research was "chicken-feed" compared to what ultimately would be needed. The oil companies are carrying out a large part of their own research and development and consider that the government should finance the research at the universities. The trouble is that the government considers that the oil companies should provide the money.

At present the Government gives £5 million for research in Scottish universities – a figure which Smith considered should be doubled or trebled to make a long-range impact on problems. In addition to this possible £10 million, industry would have to spend £20 million, with another £20 million going to Government establishments, giving a total of £50 million, which in the future could be found from profit and taxes on oil production. The profits and taxes had been estimated at £2 billion and £6 billion respectively, in the early 1980s. The possibility of £10 million being used for *new* long-range research and another £20 million for additional research in Government establishments in Scotland, from oil taxes, with the oil industry providing £10 million from profits and Scottish industry giving a similar amount, would make up the total. But *before* then there are the urgent problems to be solved to obtain oil.

There are many other areas, too, besides oil, which require long-term research, and money to allow that research to take place. (Figures issued by the Scottish Council Research Institute show that the number of people involved in research and development dropped from 8.9% in 1966 to 7.9% in 1973.

The actual number was 7,500 in 1973 compared to 49,400 in the south of England.)

Smith admitted that a small nation like Scotland could not do everything. The essential is that "something" should be done and done outstandingly well, because it is only on that basis that Scotland would be accepted as a member of the large international club which was concerned with research, not only scientific research, but in economics, sociology, medicine and a whole range of topics which are absolutely essential for the on-going economic and social well-being of any nation.

In Scotland there are a number of major research establishments sponsored by the Government, notably the National Engineering Laboratory at East Kilbride, and the Atomic Energy Research and Development Establishment at Dounreay, along with others sponsored by such organisations as the Agricultural Research Council, and the Medical Research Council. A number of companies are doing oustanding research, though industry generally is lacking in growth of research. The universities have a special role because they have an independent view and voice – absolute essentials – which were not prejudiced by commercial, political or other views and pressures.

Scotland has special needs but they had to be related to problems that concerned the U.K. as a whole, Europe, and the rest of the world.

Smith's view was based on the philosophy put forward to the Forum in a paper by Professor Hubert Curien, since 1973 Delegate-General for Technical and Scientific Research at the French Ministry for Industry and Research.

The difficulty, stated Curien, about investment in research was a psychological one which came from the impediment of valuing its benefits in the same way as for other investments. Nobody really doubted the necessity of doing research, but there was the irritation of being obliged to admit that research and development could not be considered as an investment like the others – put in so much and so much will be gained. The attitude led to ill-tempered investment, which was a bad way to invest – if some research happened to be unsuccessful (and research *had* to be sometimes unsuccessful) the investor would think he was right to be reluctant; if there was success (and it was often successful) he thought it was a miracle. Research did not deserve either the reluctance, or the belief in miracles. It did demand a special attention to its peculiar nature and possibilities, a different way of thinking investments. There was no recipe available. Science policy had only been born twenty years ago, but in that time, all the people involved in science policy had obtained useful experience, from which it had been possible to gain some ideas about investment in research. Investing in progress of knowledge never happened, historically, to be unproductive. Even if theoreticians of economics are still unable to determine exactly the role of progress in the growth of modern economics, all responsible people know how disastrous it would be for a nation to be completely dependent on others for science, how dangerous it would be for a firm to confront the national or international competitiveness of the market without new technologies. Arguments were put forward, sometimes, that a country could save a lot of its investments in basic research since the results of the whole basic research done in the world were published. The argument, according to Curien, was not only selfish, but ill-advised. To understand the results from elsewhere and make use of them it was necessary to be at the same level as the researchers who discovered them. World-wide research was a kind of a club for which the membership had to be paid.

Investing in research is very different from investing in walls, machines or any other kind of work; research work has its own rules, its peculiar demands. The most important one is demand for continuity, and consequently continuity in financial support. This is true whether it is governmental or industrial research, and it means that both rapid deceleration and acceleration in investments are equally prejudicial; rapid deceleration might happen to stop the birth of the novelty expected, rapid acceleration ran the risk of "running light".

At the government level, for instance, there were some research areas for which it would be ill-advised to increase budgets, because there were not enough good researchers available, or because there were not enough new subjects. But on the contrary, as soon as it has been decided to invest in some subject, team or laboratory, it is necessary to insure the work against discontinuity. Nothing is more prejudicial than suddenly to decide to ask research the solution of some new problem, without looking at the work in progress and for which the first investment was decided.

Research is expected to give two kind of products: results or ideas, i.e. anticipated or unanticipated novelties. An investor had certainly to order both of them, but being aware, in each case, of the game's rules. When he buys results, in order to solve some problem (theoretical or technical) he runs the risk of getting quickly obsolete results, as it happens sometimes in industrial research; moreover, such a research runs the risk of being only repetitive, because there is not any new idea to modify the approach to the issues. In the other case, when he buys ideas, first he must be richer (because an idea, as any scarce product, is long to discover and expensive); secondly he must be sure (himself) to be open-minded enough to understand the new idea and conceive its further development. That is the central issue of novelty.

By definition, novelty is a break in mental habit, it sometimes looks like an attack. The whole history of science, both basic and applied, is the history of the fight between new ideas and established ideas.

Ideas or results? That is the central issue of science policy and of research management. In a sense, it is a false dilemma because it is both impossible either to sacrifice progress of knowledge to short-term objectives (in their own interest) or to sacrifice these legitimate objectives to progress of knowledge for its own sake. In another sense, it is a true dilemma; how to co-ordinate the objectives of decision-makers (i.e. investors) which can be economic, social or even political, with the purely scientific objectives and abilities that researchers are alone to know? There is a general trend to ask basic researchers more and more firmly to learn how to catch every chance of opening their work to further applications, and to admit, on the contrary, that oriented researchers need to find new strength in some free research. There was an interesting debate about the last point in Great Britain in 1972, when Lord Rothschild, whose point of view as an investor was maybe a little too classical, admitted that 10% of the research-oriented financial support could be granted for free research.

A more real issue is opening basic research to further application. A good part of basic research has purely cultural goals and leads very rarely to outside progress, or does so after such a long time that it is absolutely impossible to programme anything. All the discoveries which were necessary to develop the transistor had, at the ultimate basis, the theory of quantas. Therefore, investing in such a basic research was for a nation an act of faith; and this is why a nation which could afford it is obliged to invest in every discipline, because nobody knows from which field decisive progress might come. On the contrary, there are some areas of basic research where a direct and spontaneous opening are more frequent: between basic biology and applied medicine or pharmacology, there were closer links than elsewhere because biologists knew clearly their possible "customers" and had many relations with them. For disciplines where these links are not self-evident attempts should be made to organise them.

Research and industry

The most expected cross-fertilisation is between research and industry. Although the situation might vary from one country to another, there is a general tendency for universities and researchers to avoid contact with industry. In Japan, contacts seem to be closer than elsewhere, and there are scientific clubs where researchers from universities and people from industrial companies meet together and look for possible common work. (If they do, the university laboratory will keep the patent for basic discovery, the company will keep the patent for the application.) In European countries patents did not seem attractive enough to overcome the reluctance of researchers. Therefore, it is perhaps a role for the State to induce university researchers to work with industrial laboratories.

Scotland's Needs

Some of the areas of research in which Scotland should at least participate in, and others which should be undertaken were outlined by Smith.

Nuclear Fission and Fusion The major *new* energy sources for the next three or four decades would be oil and gas on the one hand and nuclear energy on the other, with coal still playing an important, but diminishing, part. In the years well beyond 2000, however, nuclear fusion was likely to be the major energy resource unless society had become so changed that the energy needs decreased rather than expanded rapidly, as present trends indicated.

There is virtually no research on fusion in Scotland, though in the development of nuclear fission Scotland had played an important part. In fact Scotland generates a greater amount of its total electricity by nuclear power stations than any country in the world, and the research lead given by the experimental breeder reactor at Dounreay, and the new prototype breeder power station, has given Scotland an outstanding position in the world in nuclear science and engineering. But the view had been put forward that the breeder would not ever be needed and posed such problems of environmental contamination and even security, through its production of plutonium, that it should be abandoned. The concentration of effort, it was argued, should be put on the long-range energy provision on nuclear fusion, the concept of which was simple, but the difficulties tremendous.

The British research is based at Culham Laboratory but, because of the long development time, cuts had been made. There is now a joint research programme with European laboratories, but there is a danger that Scotland, without any share in the research, would lose talented scientists and engineers to the development taking place elsewhere.

Coal Scotland's principal energy resource of the past still has a very important part to play. With a greater need for coal than was once thought, research into new techniques of mining it economically were required, as well as dealing with the environmental aspects which were a new factor in all large scale proposals.

In fact, as Michael Parker, director of the Central Planning Unit of the National Coal Board pointed out, coal still provides over one-third of the primary energy used in Scotland. The NCB had long-term substantial investment plans based on producing coal significantly cheaper than the current international oil price, and even in Scotland, which was often popularly regarded as a high-cost coalfield, coal was being produced at less than the cost of oil. The Scottish coalfield had a very much higher proportion of new modern capacity than other coalfields in Britain.

Other Energy Sources The Scottish Hydro-Electric Board schemes provided an excellent example of the use of natural resources to meet not only local needs but also as a supplement to the national supply of electricity (though now the Board is switching new developments into conventional power stations). Other elements are being investigated, such as solar power for heat, though the cost of that so far has proved prohibitive, except for special uses in very remote areas and on artificial satellites; and the use of wind. So far nothing quantitative about the amounts of energy likely to be supplied by the "minor constituents" is available because of the lack of research.

An ambitious study was taking place in the United States into assessing for the future the best and most likely energy mix. In a very small way a similar study is being made at the Heriot-Watt University. The individual involved has excellent contacts with the team in the United States and has participated in some of the studies. But the research in Scotland was being paid for by a small contribution from four different boards, with the balance being made by the consultancy fees earned by a private individual! That kind of funding was enough to get a study *started* but the whole problem was large and serious and needed the collaborative effort of a lot of people over a number of years. The subject was so vitally important for the national prosperity both in the near and distant future that it could be argued that a central research centre concerned with energy studies should be set up in Scotland – a proposal which had been suggested before but which needed urgent implementation.

Transport and Telecommunications   A great deal of research was required into the future of the transport system, particularly with the high cost of fuel which in years to come might be prohibitive. It has to be accepted that there will continue to be a substantial amount of road transport and the problem is to find an alternative source of energy. Nuclear energy again might be the primary source, but breaking the energy down into bundles small enough to be used by individual vehicles is the difficulty which has to be overcome. Two approaches seem to be open but both required a great deal of research before they became practical.

The first is through the use of electric storage-batteries or fuel cells. Both are just marginally useful for transport at the present time, but need to be brought to a considerably higher state of efficiency and convenience before being competitive with oil. (The South of Scotland Electricity Board have been involved financially in the development at the Electricity Council Laboratories at Copenhurst of the sodium-sulphur battery for electric traction. The battery has been launched as a commercial project in conjunction with Chloride Electrical).

The second alternative was the use of nuclear power to synthesise a fuel which could be burned – the simplest being hydrogen which could be obtained in unlimited quantities by the electrolysis of water. At ordinary temperatures, however, hydrogen is a gas and the amounts to be carried would be very bulky even if under pressure. Liquid hydrogen can readily be produced by use of low-temperature techniques, but the handling problems as a fuel would be formidable. Techniques, however, have been highly developed for the space programme and use as liquid hydrogen in long-range aircraft might be possible, though economically unattractive. For road vehicles the problems are much greater. Hydrogen might have to be "bound" as in methanol or metallic hybrids – though one requires large quantities of carbon and the latter, scarce metals.

Possibly the first public suggestion in Scotland that vehicles some time in the future might be run on electrolytic hydrogen was made at the second International Forum in February 1972, by Jan de Vries, president of the Bredero Group in Holland.

But in a more general way a great deal of work is being done on the use of hydrogen power throughout the world – particularly at Ispra, the Joint Research Centre of Euratom in Italy, and at Stanford Research Institute in California.

Professor Nicoll in *A Future for Scotland* in 1973[1] suggested that Scotland should consider hydrogen energy.

Widespread research suggests that the main carrier of energy in the future will be hydrogen. Hydrogen has two principal advantages.

1. Hydrogen can be transported and stored easily without much difficulty. Thus in periods of slack demand it would be possible to store up large quantities of hydrogen in readiness for the next peak period, and so there would never be a situation where the demand for fuel exceeds the supply. Large scale storage could be undertaken in geological structures such as exhausted natural gas fields. The pipeline grid when developed would have considerable storage capacity and local storage would be possible after liquefaction.

2. When burned, hydrogen reverts to water from which it is produced and thus it is a completely non-pollutive re-cyclable

1 *A Future for Scotland*, pp. 57, 58, 59: Ronald E. Nicoll: Scottish Council.

fuel. This will be very important as measures to control pollution are strengthened, and the environmental problems associated with the generation, distribution and use of energy by existing methods become increasingly unacceptable.

Pipeline transport costs of hydrogen are slightly higher than those for natural gas, for which there already exists an extensive network in Western Europe. During a transitional stage hydrogen could be mixed with methane for distribution, which would help to slow down the depletion of natural gas resources.

Despite a relatively high price at present, hydrogen is already being used extensively in chemical plants, petroleum refineries and steelworks. World production is running at 200 thousand million cubic metres a year, with West European production expected to rise from 40 to 100 thousand million cubic metres in 1980. On a calorific value basis, hydrogen produced by conventional processes in Western Europe is about three times as expensive as natural gas. But according to a calculation by Euratom the cost could be cut by half in new processes. As the price of energy in general is bound to go up, hydrogen could soon become competitive.

The use of hydrogen in certain industrialised regions is already so widespread that pipeline networks have been built for its transport. One such network links various plants in the Rhine-Ruhr area, covering a total pipeline distance of 190 kilometres. Similar distribution networks exist in the U.S.A., notably in Texas. The Soviet Union have installed an electrolytic plant on the Aswan Dam in Egypt, which seems to work perfectly (it is not known what they have operating in their own country).

There is also a pipeline network for the distribution of oxygen to industrial plants in Western Europe, running from France into West Germany, Luxembourg and Belgium.

Because transporting hydrogen is relatively cheap (approximately one-twelfth of the cost of transporting electricity) the distance it can be moved to the market will be much greater. Hydrogen could become a major form of energy, being produced in large-scale remote nuclear plants and supplied to the population centres over long distances in international pipeline grids such as are developing in Europe for gas.

All this depends on developing a reasonably cheap process of breaking up water. The aim is to evolve a method of splitting water into its main components, namely hydrogen and oxygen without the use of fossil fuels or electricity. Today, hydrogen for industrial processes comes primarily from natural gas – one of the very fossil fuels it is hoped to replace. Electrolysis, (passing through water) although expensive has already been given practical application in Russia. Hydrogen can also be produced from coal, but this again means using up one valuable fuel to produce another.

A new process is being devised at Ispras. It has the advantage of only using water and nuclear heat as its raw materials. Thermal cracking of water requires temperatures of 2,500–3,000°C – limits well beyond present-day nuclear reactors. Ispra have been trying to solve the problem by using the available temperatures of less than 800°C together with catalytic processes. The by-products of the ensuing chemical reactions are hydrogen and oxygen (this could be used in the gasification of coal in blast furnaces and steelworks).

There appear to be three major problems which must be overcome before one could confidently predict the development of this type of energy system:

1. A process of producing hydrogen cheaply must be perfected.

2. If the process is dependent on the use of large-scale nuclear plants then the problems of building such plants must be overcome.

3. Nuclear plants must be run at a steady and continuous rate. Therefore very large quantities of energy would have to be stored to cope with fluctuations in demand.

Implications for Scotland of the Development of Hydrogen Systems If these problems can be overcome then Scotland could play a significant role as a source of this new type of energy for Britain and perhaps other parts of Western Europe.

In Scotland there are available remote areas with rocky coast-lines and deep water close to shore, suitable for the location of large nuclear plant. This would reduce the need to build power stations in already over-industrialised areas where shortages of suitable sites and problems associated with the loss of amenity are particularly acute.

By 1990, as the result of the exploitation of oil and gas reserves in the sea beds around Scotland, there will almost certainly be a highly developed pipeline system linking many parts of Scotland to the major markets of the south and probably Western Europe. This pipeline grid could easily be adapted to serve as a hydrogen grid, so that markets at a distance could be supplied at reasonable cost. The other method of transporting gases such as hydrogen is in a liquid form in bulk carriers, and Scotland's deep water harbour potential could be exploited for this.

The oil and gas discoveries in the North Sea and the development of the Oceanspan concept will probably have led to the creation in Scotland by 1990 of major complexes of processing industries which will be very energy-intensive and which will create a strong local demand.

The development of hydrogen as a major energy carrier could assist in maintaining the economic expansion which will result from the present activity in the North Sea and the development of the Hunterston peninsula, particularly steel-making. As thermal power stations have an over-capacity, even using electrolytical splitting of water the storage of hydrogen could be competitive. Given enough confidence in the future of hydrogen, the over-capacity in thermal power stations could provide an opportunity for an experimental trial of a large scale hydrogen system.

For these reasons there is a strong case for Scotland becoming deeply involved in the research programme at present under way on the Continent.

(Since the above was published, Strathclyde University has set up an energy group under Dr Malcolm Slessor and has been involved in discussions about becoming involved in research into hydrogen power. It is expected that money for the research in which Strathclyde would co-operate with the Joint Research Centre at Ispra and Stanford will be provided by the EEC.)

The future for much of the movement of heavy transport between main centres had to lie in the use of the railways. But the transfer of goods between rail and road vehicles still presented problems. Support for research into the road-rail transfer system came from David Cobbet, the general manager of British rail in Scotland.

The freightliner system, which was a British innovation, still leads the world but it has not quite developed as expected because of the inability, to date, to combine road-rail transfer in the most expeditious and economic way. The system at present being used, overhead cranes, was expensive and slightly unreliable and there was a great need for research into the problems.

In telecommunications there was a requirement for a more widespread sophisticated system.

"It should not always be necessary for three people to travel from Oban, Inverness and Edinburgh to meet a fourth in Glasgow!"

Some outstanding research in communications has been carried out in Scotland, with the part played by Scottish industry in the whole electronics field. But there is too much dependence on new techniques developed elsewhere.

Agriculture and Fishing Both are basic industries of Scotland, with agriculture being the largest single industry.

Though Smith considered that encouragement for imaginative thinking on the maximum use of land was important, it was another type of research that Maitland Mackie, chairman of the North East of Scotland Development Authority considered essential – research into managing the agricultural market. Milk marketing is one of the best examples of an organised market which has been of benefit to the producer and the consumer, not only in Britain but in other parts of the world.

What is required was a similar approach to beef and cereals. The farming industry could undoubtedly produce more if people are willing to pay, but it is impossible for the individual farmer to really aim for maximum production when a very small surplus could create havoc on the market – the type of havoc which has occurred in beef.

Research in fishing usually meant better ways of landing catches and this led to a depletion of stocks, said Smith. But he thought there was an urgent need for research into fish-farming to provide food. In fact, both the Herring Industry Board and the White Fish Authority do have research which includes the problem of conservation. (In 1975 it has been agreed by the North Eastern Atlantic Fisheries Convention that herring fishing will not take place around the Faroes and in Arctic waters where spawning takes place to allow an increase in the numbers.) Both bodies also do a considerable amount of work, employing scientists, on research into marketing.

On forestry, James Bruce, vice chairman of the British Forestry Committee and a member of the national board of the Scottish Woodland Owners Association, wanted to see funds for research and development into discovering the uses for carbon created by photosynthesis in timber. One theory, he revealed, has been put forward by a director of the National Gas Production Research Establishment that a 30 sq. mile forest could synthesise the U.K.'s complete kerosene and aviation fuel need.

Fundamental Science Investigations for their own sake – as opposed to "applied research" – could not be ignored because from it had come some of the most far-reaching advances. Scotland could not deal with *every* field but there should be some well-chosen fields in which investment should be made. Support would not only cover the physical and biological sciences but also the social sciences and the arts. The cost would be small compared with "applied research" but the results in the long-term might be even more valuable. Smith did not attempt to detail the areas of fundamental science. His view was that it was necessary to attempt to identify individuals with ideas and assist them.

Health and Happiness Scotland has a world reputation for the excellence of its medical research and practice and every effort has to be made to maintain it with money and brain-power. The emphasis should be on preventive medicine rather than the cure of ill-health. Innovation in preventive medicine and psychiatry is a world-wide business, but in researching some of the ailments in Scotland – the higher than average incidence in respiratory and rheumatic complaints; the high rate of lung cancer in the West of Scotland; and multiple sclerosis which is three times the U.K. average in the north of Scotland – causes might be found which would prevent such diseases else-where.

Two strong criticisms of Smith's views were made – (1) that to attempt to have the research done in Scotland did not recognise that research did not have any boundaries, (2) his special pleading for research to be done in the universities with adequate funds provided.

The attitude expressed by Francis Tombs of the SSEB was echoed by others. "There is no frontier which prevents the transfer of information from the South (England) to the North (Scotland), and what one ought to do is choose the centre which is best equipped to do the research on a particular subject. If research is regarded as an in-put to industry, that is the only consideration. If the location of research from the point of view of providing job opportunities for new graduates is being considered then there may be other arguments. But from the point of view of research influence on industry its location is irrelevant."

But the critics had appeared not to take notice of Curien's philosophy – or have dismissed it as being peculiarly French – that "world-wide research is a kind of club of which you have to pay for membership". The same argument applies more or less for an industrial company. It could buy patents, but it was good to be able to understand them, and even better to discover its own new technology and sell it. That appeared to be the spirit behind Smith's arguments.

Tombs again encapsulated some of the feelings about using universities for research work, though he tempered it by stating that the results of work done had been satisfactory. The problem, however, is that most of the work done at universities was by post-graduate students who were tied to their own time-scale – either to produce a thesis or obtain a higher degree – and if it did not happen to fit the project then the work was only half-done.

Dr Neville Woodward, an International Research Policy and Management Adviser who presented his views on "Thinking Agencies" (see next Chapter) was fairly blunt about the position of universities.

"We should not forget that their main function is to teach. The universities are certainly sources of ideas and should certainly be made use of in that respect. In general terms I do not think the university's job is to undertake research under contract for industry. Looked at world-wide, universities even in America have not really made a success of research as a business. One finds a post-graduate student with not very much experience doing the work supervised by a professor who is terribly busy."

He accused Smith of being like so many of his professorial colleagues who tend to follow what Woodward regarded as the British establishment idea which had dominated official British thinking on research and development since 1946 – pump more and more money into government research establishments, into the universities, and beat the backs of industry hoping that they would spend more and more money in their own industrial laboratories.

"The day is past," said Woodward, "when one could say 'research is good for you'. It has to be justified now by a hard, cold financial look."

chapter 8

Thinking
Agencies

Over many years pleas have been made to successive governments for the establishment of more research units in Scotland.

Three main reasons have been behind attempts to influence governments to attach more importance to the need – a possible stemming of any "brain drain" among university graduates to other parts of Britain or abroad; the possible attraction of industrial development near any such units; the encouragement to industrial firms to create research and development groups in Scottish based plants.

The efforts have been spectacularly unsuccessful despite the fact that the situation, according to Neville Woodward, is "almost too incredible to believe".

Woodward is advising the Scottish Council in his capacity as an international research policy and management adviser in its bid to create a Scottish "think tank" – an agency which would be creative and innovative. In recent years he has been studying science policy and research and development in about 30 countries throughout the world. In 1957 he was one of two people largely responsible for instigating the arrival in Scotland of the well-known American Arthur D. Little Research Institute, which in 1970 became the Inveresk Research International (after buying out the American influence) – a private non-profit making body which undertakes research under contract for industry, governments and international organisations and employs 150 people near Edinburgh.

Woodward's "hard, cold financial look" at research includes what he regards as the need for integrated planning – technical, sociological, and economic – backed by cost-benefit studies, and a critical examination of techniques to make research and development more creative and innovative and make fewer demands on scarce scientific manpower and money.

If his attitude towards the universities is slightly scathing, his view of Britain's national research and development policy is one of contempt.

Britain spends more of its Gross National Product on research and development, 2.4%, than any country in Europe and brings forth the rather caustic comment from Woodward:

"It has produced scintillating and excellent research the like of which is found hardly anywhere else in the world. It has produced a number of Fellows of the Royal Society, and a few Nobel Laureates. It has produced ideas for others to develop. But from the point of view of the national economy it has not paid off. We pay more *per capita* than any other country in Europe and we are near the bottom of the economic league."

The Government's part in supporting research and development in Scotland is worse than the bad situation in Britain. Apart from the research on the fast-breeder reactor at the Dounreay atomic plant, there are 17 Government financed or controlled laboratories in Scotland – but only one, the National Engineering Laboratory at East Kilbride – was specifically set up to assist manufacturing industry. Fifteen are concerned with agriculture, fisheries and biology and the remaining one with geology.

Out of the 42 Government industry research associations and the 14 research institutes not one is in Scotland – though Woodward's view is that nothing innovative, outside agriculture and fisheries, has resulted from the institutes in the past thirty years.

The main reason for this neglect of Scotland is that all the thinking is done in Whitehall, and the Government is not going to move any of the associations and the institutes from their present locations.

153

"Think Tank" Background

In Scotland, as elsewhere, innovation by individuals have been replaced more and more by the team approach to the solution of specific problems or development of new products and processes usually backed by sophisticated equipment and extremely expensive laboratories and workshops. Scotland's technological thinking and development, like other parts of Britain, has been over the last thirty years almost entirely in the hands of scientists, technologists and economists in industry, government and the universities. Only with the Inveresk Research International has an independent contract research organisation appeared in Scotland.

IRI is an excellent example of what could be done in a difficult field without government-financed help. Against all advice to the contrary, it has succeeded in building up an international research and development business and reputation without recourse to taxpayers money.

The reasons for its success has been mainly because it filled a need and looked for support outside, as well as within Scotland; it had been able to call on the experience of international experts (Arthur D. Little); it had a strong board, good management, staff and facilities; and it was free from the "deadening hand" of the Civil Service. In addition, it was flexible, innovative, able to make quick decisions, and act with speed and keep in constant touch with the market place.

Four of Scotland's universities, Strathclyde in Glasgow, Heriot-Watt and Edinburgh and Stirling, operate units to liaise with industry or seek support in the form of research contracts. The last three universities have units which in effect are co-ordinating and liaison offices whose job is to obtain research contracts and place them with the most appropriate department within the university.

"None of them has been particularly successful", said Woodward. "One of the reasons for this apparently is the desire of many professors to make personal consultancy arrangements direct with industrial and other sponsors."

The Strathclyde Centre of Industrial Innovation was a far more ambitious operation than the others and was part of a Government scheme to develop industrial units in selected universities. About £500,000, half of which was in the form of a government grant, was spent on laboratories and workshops but the operations virtually collapsed when the government subsidy ran out.

Any real innovative successes in Scottish universities, asserted Woodward, such as electrical engineering (Edinburgh), offshore engineering (Heriot-Watt), desalination (Glasgow), bioengineering and fish farming (Strathclyde) had stemmed from the skills and enthusiasm of individual professors.

Though Scotland has a considerable number of research establishments – governmental, university and independent with a number of firms with research departments – few can be looked on as "thinking agencies". There is not in any way a national "think tank".

The question which has still to be answered – and the Scottish Council is continuing its pursuit of the idea – is, what kind of "think tank" was wanted in Scotland? Is it to be a "creative" operation which is primarily innovative and entrepreneurial (the American "think tank" type of organisation) or a "service" organisation, such as a new research institute to cover a specific field such as energy. The latter could be planned and organised provided the money and skilled manpower was available while the former could not.

Creative Agencies Although many attempts had been made in many parts of the world, nobody, so far, had succeeded in finding a formula for inducing "creativity", or an ability to innovate, or for assessing it, in individuals or organisations.

Nevertheless, some communities have more creativity than others and as far as technology is concerned over the last 50 years the leaders have been the United States. There were three types of corporate thinking agencies in the United States:

1. "Think Tanks" of which the best known were the Rand Corporation and Tempo, financed and controlled by large

industrial companies whose long-term interests they serve, and the Hudson Institute and Resources for the Future Inc., both of which are privately financed and completely independent of, and not subject to, pressures from government, industry, the banks or universities. Rand, Tempo and Hudson all have a high-calibre, multi-disciplinary staff who devote their energies, mostly under relaxed conditions, to anticipating the problems of the year 2000 and later, and working out possible solutions. All are involved in technological forecasting.

2. Independent contract research institutes which work for industrial companies. The rapid development of sponsored research in the United States has probably been due to an early awareness of the important part research plays in industrial development and during the last thirty years a belief that industrial research is the proper function and responsibility of industry and not of the government. The "big three", Battelle Memorial Institute, Stanford Research Institute and Arthur D. Little in 1970 collectively employed 8,000 scientists, technologists and economists and supporting staff and earned $190 million in fees. Canada and Korea also have institutes on similar lines. In Britain there are several successful research laboratories but all concentrate on laboratory work and do not provide multi-disciplinary i.e. science, technology, economics, management, services, as do Stanford and other American institutes.

3. Specialist Foundations such as Rockefeller and Ford are mainly concerned with financing creative projects in existing organisations rather than being creative themselves.

Though the corporate thinking agencies have made an impact in the U.S. the greatest technological-commercial successes have been in industrial laboratories e.g. nylon (Dupont), transistors (Bell Telephone) tetra ethyl lead (General Motors) and others, which have combined entrepreneurship with a hard-headed commercial approach.

A similar though not so impressive list could be made of British inventors who have been commercially successful with terylene, penicillin, polyethylene, though none of them have been in Scotland, which has been dependent in the last twenty years on imported technology and know-how.

Britain does not have the independent American "think tank". The Government's Central Policy Review Unit headed by Lord Rothschild and the Programme Analysis Unit at Harwell are both concerned more with economic assessment of government programmes, technological and otherwise, than with creative thinking or technological forecasting. The Scottish Office's regional development organisation which covers economic planning, industrial development, regional development policy, economics and statistics could be a "thinking agency" but is rather more a conventional government department, mainly concerned with the implementation of decisions.

There are "think tanks" of the American-type in some of the private and nationalised industries. The Steel Corporation has a permanent unit which concerns itself with long range planning which involves forecasting steel usage during the rest of the century. ICI has a long-range planning group which amongst other projects has undertaken a long-range forecasting exercise entitled "ICI in the year 2000" and attempts to anticipate what a city would be like and the problems it would have in the twenty-first century.

Woodward had suggested to the Scottish Council that a co-ordinating "thinking agency" might be the easiest to initiate, staff and operate than a corporate "thinking agency", and was more likely to give quick results and be considerably cheaper to run.

One of the co-ordinating "thinking agencies" which might be used as an example is the International Development Research Centre (IDRC) based in Ottawa. Set up six years ago partly at the instigation of the Canadian International Development Administration and started with an endowment of $30 million, its main purpose is to involve universities in developed countries in tackling developing-country industrial and technical problems. The main interest to Scotland is in the method of operation. IDRC's headquarters are in Ottawa headed by a director who has a small resident staff. The Centre had five operating divisions whose heads are not all Canadians or based at Ottawa. IDRC's policy is to identify the person whom they think best suited to the job and invite him, backed by the organisation which employs him, to serve as a division head on a part time basis. One division head is an Englishman, normally located at the University of Sussex near Brighton. The technique has been found to be very effective in practice and if applied in Scotland could utilise the part-time services of experts in existing research organisations in Scotland or elsewhere.

"There is little doubt that there has long been a need for one or more 'thinking agencies' in Scotland oriented towards Scotland's needs, present and future, and under non-governmental control," said Woodward.

The British government's machine has failed to produce any new creative organisations in Scotland over the past thirty years and such innovative bodies and activities as have emerged during the period have resulted from the efforts of individuals, either on their own or through the medium of such independent bodies as the universities, a few forward looking firms, or the Scottish Council.

Those bursts of creative activity had been sporadic and unco-ordinated and in many cases had atrophied due to lack of support, guidance, enthusiasm or understanding from, or by, the "establishment".

With the growing realisation that Scotland had enormous potential, both of educated manpower and resources, with the likelihood of significant income resulting from the exploitation of North Sea oil the time was ripe for serious consideration to be given to the establishment of one or more "thinking agencies" in Scotland.

The first decision to be made will have regard to the number and type of "thinking agencies" which could and should be established, having in mind Scotland's present and future needs, the organisations already functioning and the availability of finance and appropriate manpower.

Woodward suggested that consideration could profitably be given to the following –

A Scottish Development Research Organisation which would be officially approved but independent, which would have the task of drawing up a "development research" programme aimed at opening up new outlets for Scottish skills and people in the years ahead, and empowered to have the programme carried out by appropriate "research" organisations already operating in Scotland and elsewhere. The Governing Board, which would not be large, would be made up of people of national, or international standing with the requisite knowledge and experience, who would give their services free. Experience suggests that to be effective the Civil Service and the universities would only have a minority representation on the Board; industrialists with a technical-economic background and working research directors were more likely to have a realistic approach, and be able to provide the drive and ability to follow through. The non-executive board would be concerned only with policy programmes and finance.

A small permanent secretariat would be set up to implement the Board's plans, with a director, and a part-time scientific counsellor attached.

The programme would be divided into appropriate categories with the division heads answerable to the director. The IDRC technique of employing part-time division heads located elsewhere would be worth trying, as not only would it save skilled manpower but also get more people and organisations involved in the execution of the programme.

Two methods of financing the research projects farmed out to existing organisations would have to be considered. The most attractive from every point of view is that the participating body pays for its share of the programme out of its own budget. The alternative and more usual method is that operated by IDRC British Research Councils whereby each research project is financed by the contracting organisation – in this case SCODRO.

It is axiomatic that SCODRO could only be effective if

the necessary skilled manpower and finance were available.

A Scottish "Stanford Research Institute" Although there are several well established and reputable independent research institutes and management consultancies in Britain there are no broadly-based multi-purpose – technical, economic, and management – organisations comparable with Stanford, Battelle and Arthur D. Little in the U.S.A., or even KIST in Korea.

It would be a formidable task to attempt to start one from scratch but consideration might be given to expanding an existing organisation of this type. The only one in Scotland is Inveresk Research International.

A specially created "think tank" on the American pattern would not be appropriate to Scotland's needs, particularly as the high quality specialist staff which would be required could be better employed by a SCODRO or a Scottish "Stanford RI".

In general, British applied or industrial research institutes stand comparison with any in the developed world.

Assuming that further institutes of this type were required in Scotland, and that the necessary skills and finance were available, consideration might first be given to what area of activity or topic is the proposed applied research institute to cover and what organisational structure and *modus-operandi* is best suited to the needs of the proposed institute?

Experiences abroad and elsewhere in Britain, provide possible guidelines to those charged with making a decision on two points. One would assume that the Scottish Council with its background and experience in, and knowledge of, the Scottish industrial scene would be able to draw up a short list of topics/areas of potential importance, which should warrant the setting up of a new applied research institute from which one could be selected at the outset.

A front runner would obviously be the proposed Energy Research Institute, but it is doubtful if a Scottish National Resources Research Institute so frequently advocated in the past is appropriate under present day conditions.

If the Scottish Council felt that it did not have sufficient information on which to base a choice it should consider the possibility of undertaking, or having undertaken by appropriate consultants, a survey of Scottish industry to assess its long-term research and technical needs.

A good example of how this can be done is to be found in the setting up of the Korea Institute of Science and Technology (KIST) in 1968. A team of twenty Korean industrial scientists guided by a three man team from Battelle Memorial Institute, Columbus, Ohio, visited all 600 secondary manufacturing companies in the Republic over a period of eighteen months and on the basis of their findings KIST was established to meet the current and future needs of Korean industry; KIST is now the most successful contract-research institute in the Far East and stands comparison with its long established American counterparts.

In Britain when a new research institute is being considered, inevitably and automatically the government is turned to as a source of finance and direction. In the U.S.A., on the contrary, first consideration is always given to private enterprise sponsorship which is one reason for the phenomenal growth of the commercial – but usually non-profit – contract laboratories such as Battelle, Stanford Research and Arthur D. Little.

Sir Alec Cairncross when he was Head of the Government Economic Services said that "the attempts of the government to pose as promoters of technological advance is in my judgment largely spoof – neither government research establishments nor the public sector as a whole can take much credit for the technological improvements upon which the rise in living standard over the past half century rests".

As the finance for any new service "Thinking Agency" that may be established in Scotland in the future is likely to come from the public purse, the best means of handling this should be considered. It is generally agreed that the most effective method is to appoint an independent Board of Management (the members of which give their part-time services without remuneration) who are concerned only with policy, over-all financial responsibility and the appointment of a Director who is solely responsible for the day-to-day operations of the institute set up and operated with the funds made available. In the case of a government-funded operation, appropriate government departments usually have assessors on the Board who serve in an advisory capacity, but who have neither executive powers nor a vote.

The activities and organisation of three quite dissimilar bodies are being examined.

Universities It was doubtful if the techniques of the four universities (already mentioned) would be made more effective by pressure from outside.

"University teachers in general are individualistic and jealously guard their academic freedom," said Woodward, "In fact, history is against them, in that few universities, even in America, have made a real success of carrying out research as a business."

The relationship between the universities and particularly the *Techniche hochschule* and industry in Switzerland and Germany, was much closer and more effective than elsewhere, but it was difficult to see how the basic philosophy on which the association was based in those countries could be applied to British universities without a revolutionary change in their thinking.

There had been several "bright ideas" of potential or actual value to industry from Scottish universities in recent years. There might be others hidden away in university departments, although the experience of National Research Development Council suggested that this was unlikely, and one of the problems would be to identify and assess the potential of these "growing points".

Royal Society of Edinburgh is Scotland's oldest and most prestigious scientific society. Fellowship of the Society is highly regarded and five times as many candidates are put forward annually as are accepted. Most of the 800 Fellows are from academiae, its lectures are well attended, its library in constant use, its "house" impressive, yet its impact upon Scottish affairs negligible.

Some years ago the Society approached the late Lord Fleck for suggestions as to how it could be made more effective; he complied with its request but nothing was done to implement his ideas. Later, the Society's membership was asked for ideas, but again nothing was done; the *status quo* won the day. Obviously it would be difficult to bring about a fundamental change but attempts might be made specifically to persuade the Society's Council to examine the structure and *modus operandi* of the Royal Swedish Academy of Engineering Sciences (IVA) to see if any of the techniques it has developed so successfully could be used with benefit by the Society. Failing that, the Scottish Council itself might consider the feasibility of adopting some of IVA's functions. It was founded in 1919 as a non-profit organisation, with the dual function of a learned society and a clearing house for research ideas of value to industry with funds for sponsoring research, often carried out in company laboratories. It was recognised as the competent body to advise Swedish government authorities and industry on action required to develop technical research and ensure its application.

Its uniqueness lies in that it has a maximum of 230 elected members below 65 years of age, all of whom hold distinguished positions at universities, in industry or in government administration, and that these members are organised in eleven sections, each holding 2–4 meetings a year.

These sections cover a wide range of industrial technology, mechanical, shipbuilding and aeronautical sciences; electro-technical, building, chemical, basic mining and metallurgical engineering, and forestry, forest product sciences; production engineering, economics, biotechnics and research planning and administration. Through these meetings and other contacts, the Academy maintains a continuous survey of the entire technological field, thus being able at any stage to detect meaningful new developments, important trends, urgent needs and present suggestions for new activities through committees and working groups.

IVA also undertakes investigations and surveys, mainly at the suggestion of members. Firstly these are pre-project studies in which ideas and suggestions are sifted, and secondly the actual carrying out of investigations with the object of producing suggestions or starting new projects. These latter are usually undertaken by existing organisations working with the Academy, but if such bodies do not exist IVA can, and does, activate new organisations for the purpose. Examples of completed projects and those in train are: environmental problems; deep freezing; use of natural gas; applied mathematics; futures research; market research and re-cycling of wastes. It also has a very effective information service, which brings to the attention of the Swedish government authorities, industrial enterprises and research institutes, knowledge of new technology, of the results of research and new ideas on matters of national importance relating to industry and engineering science.

Research Parks There are three Research Parks in Scotland all within 25 miles of each other – Riccarton (Heriot-Watt University), Glenrothes and Livingston – each operating under a different agency and none has been particularly successful.

The reasons for this lack of success are not hard to find: (i) The idea is foreign to Britain (ii) the three agencies concerned failed to discuss their plans with each other (iii) no market surveys were carried out before launching the "Park" and (iv) the techniques used to attract research organisations to these Parks, and once there to maintain their interest, have in the main been amateurish. Also no attempt appears to have been made to apply U.S.A./Canadian experience.

There is obviously a case for only one Research Park in southern Scotland operated by people with industrial experience who would retain a competent firm of estate agents to "sell" the Park to potential customers. In other words, for success, a Research Park had to be treated as a commercial and not as a university or governmental venture.

Sir Frederick Stewart, Regius Professor of Geology at Edinburgh and chairman of the advisory Board for Research Councils disagreed with Woodward's "cold, hard financial look" at research and thinking in terms of benefit analyses. The attitude was one of "basic research is a fine game for those who indulge in it but it is really not of much use, and it is a luxury we cannot afford."

Clearly there were limits to what could be afforded in basic research and the U.K. had not been good at translating into economic benefits some of the better ideas from basic research. But to attempt to quantify the benefits of basic research did not allow for the complexity of the network and for the unpredictability of the results – and unpredictability and unquantifiable benefits were anathema to some of those who held the "purse strings". The results were extremely important, said Stewart, as most of the economic progress had been achieved from the very large input from both basic and applied research.

As an example, he cited the North Sea oil exploration which had taken place as a result of basic geological and geophysical research by an enormous number of people working on a "curiosity basis" which had stimulated applied researchers, who then again stimulated the basic researchers, who did the same again. There was a tendency to forget that it was not only positive results of research which were important, but the negative ones – a prediction where there was *not* an oil-bearing structure – which could be of value.

"We must invest in all parts of the network and in the people who are training to come in to all parts of the network and research must be carried on, not only in institutes but in universities where it is associated with training, where students learn not only how to tackle some problems but something at the forefront of the science that they are studying.

"If all the people coming out of universities were tailor-made for industry of a particular kind then it would lead to the stultification of industry because they would be exactly like all the people who are already there. One does really need to take in people who are not altogether popular, but who are capable of criticising what is already happening."

There is one improvement in the network which might be made. Often university workers are intent only on their own particular line and had results which could be of importance to industry. The workers might not be aware of it, and industry would not be aware of it. Industrial people might consider the possibility of visiting universities more than they did on the basis of finding out what is going on. At the same time, it would be helpful both to the universities and industry if lecturers in science, or in some branches of the subject, spent a year in industry.

Sir Patrick Thomas, chairman of the Scottish Transport Group, who is also a member of the Strathclyde University Court, pointed out, however, that most universities had to spend a great deal of their time thinking about money. The universities had two functions – to teach and to do research. But more discipline, because of the financial situation, has to be applied in the allocation of the resources. It was fashionable for all academics to say that all knowledge was useful, but efforts had to be made to be more selective, particularly with project research – the short-term study which might produce quick answers to immediate problems. He admitted, as Woodward had stated, that the Centre of Industrial Innovation at Strathclyde had not been as successful as had been hoped.

Woodward agreed with Stewart over the suggestion that university lecturers should spend some time in industry at some stage in their career, but he still held to his views about the British approach to research and development.

"Someone with one of the research councils said recently that it was essential for a nation to have a scientific policy, but it was imperative that the policy be not implemented. This is a particularly British approach which I do not go along with at all."

Note: The Scottish Council is going ahead with a plan to outline a research policy for Scotland. Discussions with various organisations, universities and the Government will take place during 1975 with a view to taking action in the future.

chapter 9

Industry and the Community

"How necessary is it to integrate research effort to benefit both industry and the community?" was the question posed by trade unionist John Boyd.

A member of the general council of the Trades Union Congress, Boyd has been since 1953 a member of the executive council of Britain's second largest union, the Amalgamated Union of Engineering Workers. In 1963–64 he was president of the Confederation of Shipbuilding and Engineering Unions and is still a member of the executive council of that body, and between 1965 and 1967 was chairman of the British Labour Party.

In attempting to answer the question posed he put forward several others.

If it intended to utilise research ideas and their finds to great advantage, what constitutes effective research and how is it best initiated? Should some thought not be given to a re-examination of the approach to research as well as considera-tion to some of the attitudes which might well be misconceived? To what extent does pre-conditioning of social and economic strata influence attitudes and reactions, as well as interest and acceptance of ideas? It was advantageous to produce and dis-seminate research data which would be of the most value. But to what extent could conflict of interests be reconciled? Pre-judice might well inhibit decisions to contain areas of research and statistics were well known for being manipulated to get desired results.

A basic point which needed to be resolved was how to overcome the many difficulties that arose in attempting to integrate research activities and ideas. During the past few decades, research activities had expanded and become more diversified as society had become more complex. Often one area of research had been unaware of what had been happening in another – the result was a piecemeal approach to research at a time when it had become increasingly vital to coordinate and integrate research findings.

The answer might be in the setting up of a Central Information and Research Centre as a "clearing house" for research data and ideas.

"It is my view," said Boyd, "that where applicable the broader spheres of research should be expected to incorporate such factors as social, industrial, economic, psychological and political points."

The strong ties of Scotland with the United Kingdom and its close association with Europe and many other countries is relevant to development. It would be incongruous if their experience and expertise were not drawn upon.

Over the years in Scotland and the United Kingdom there has been a tendency to wait until an adverse situation arose before attempting to rectify it. Under these circumstances that had meant patching and repair-work which could never get to the root of the problem. In 1974 the *Financial Times* in an article about Scotland stated:

"Scotland's institutional representatives – those of industry and finance houses, among its trade unions and development agencies and within Government – have become conditioned by the need to seek ways out of economic difficulties rather than ways into the economic opportunities."

Stated Boyd: "The derelict and depressive conditions which still exist in some parts of West Central Scotland are a monument to misjudgment as well as insufficient planning. What a price to pay for experience! It is necessary, therefore, to probe and rethink on finding the best way to tackle such problems and through planning and research make sure no such travesties will ever again appear on the Scottish horizon."

The Scottish Council's basic guidelines provided common aims – solve unemployment; stop emigration by providing gifted Scots with opportunities at home; plan carefully in land use; develop national resources (maximise potential and minimise destruction).

To maximise potential it would be fair to look at the recent past, consider the present, and plan for a prosperous future, drawing substantially from new ideas and research jointly arrived at by assimilating and co-ordinating knowledge gained over the years, in industry, the community and elsewhere, hopefully avoiding repeating errors, while incorporating what had proved successful.

What Boyd was really seeking was to find out to what extent people are willing to live above sectional interest and adopt an attitude towards research based on seeking, not their own personal gratification or their own personal interests, but the addition of as many benefits as possible to industry and the community.

Trade Union Ideas In 1974 the Scottish Trade Union Congress adopted the following as policy –

1. The government should play a specifically interventionist role in financing and management of industry including where necessary:
(a) direction of industry to areas of persistent unemployment and low growth performance
(b) establishment of state-owned enterprises in the area.

2. Establishment of a Scottish Development Authority which would:
(a) co-ordinate planning
(b) have power over land acquisition and finance
(c) set up a Scottish State Holding Company which could buy into firms where jobs are in jeopardy.

Scotland's Minister of State Bruce Millan spoke about the role of the Scottish Development Agency and what the Government hoped to achieve through it. (See note p. 186.)

It was intended through the Agency to devote extra resources to tackle the regeneration of those parts of Scotland which were still suffering from the legacy of the last industrial revolution, and might not, without Government action, benefit fully from the new revolution created by oil development. Money would be made available even before oil revenues provided an appreciable measure of relief to the difficult public expenditure situation. The Government were according an extremely high priority to the needs of Scotland for redevelopment.

"It is imperative that we make a start right away on regenerating the industry and the environment of older industrial areas, especially in West Central Scotland, whose problems have emerged with increasing clarity over recent years as the most acute which Scotland has to tackle.

In the past ten years there has been a marked deterioration in the relative position of West Central Scotland and the tendency is being reinforced by the pattern of development associated with North Sea oil."

The most revealing indicator has been the emigration figures. West Central Scotland's share of emigration loss from Scotland rose from about 60% to over 70% through the 1960s. Today it is the only region losing population by migration. In 1972–73 when all other regions gained, the outflow of population from West Central Scotland continued unabated. Figures for the 12 months up to June 1974 indicated that there was a net gain of population in Scotland of about 5,000 – the largest inflow of people to Scotland in 40 years (excluding 1939–45).

Though the West Central region is losing workers, unlike the 1960s, it appears they are finding the job opportunities in the North and East of Scotland instead of going abroad or to England.

"This is a very definite gain for Scotland as a whole," was Millan's view. "But the progressive loss of a substantial and ambitious element of the potential working force, which West

Central Scotland has sustained over the post-war period, cannot continue indefinitely if that region, which contains half of Scotland's population and 60% of its industrial capacity, is to provide the basis of a balanced and prosperous economy. The notion of newly prosperous Scotland had no validity unless it had a balanced prosperity, in the same way that prosperity for the U.K. could never be achieved if only the South East of England were prosperous. It was for this reason that the Government was not prepared simply to concentrate its attentions on supporting the development of the regions most affected by oil development, but would give equal and urgent priority to the older industrial areas especially in the West Central region.

The new Scottish Development Agency will have as its primary task the regeneration of such areas, which will spearhead the Government's programme for the modernisation and growth of industry and for the creation of a modern and attractive environment in which industry and its workpeople can flourish. The industrial opportunities created by off-shore oil markets would continue to be, as they had already proved to be, an important catalyst for industry redevelopment. In the environmental field, the Agency would be able to work with powerful new partners in the shape of the newly organised local authorities. It would work closely with them, providing extra resources to speed up the clearance of industrial and urban dereliction.

Millan admitted that the injection of Government money on its own, whether through the Scottish Development Agency or in other ways, would not provide the complete solution. New prosperity would not be created without change – in markets and technology, jobs and environment. Government, industrialists, workers and citizens had to welcome change, not uncritically, but positively. An automatic resistance to change, an adherence to current ways for their own sake, was a recipe for failure.

Maitland Mackie, chairman of the North East Scotland Development Association highlighted perhaps one of the problems in Scotland – the proliferation of agencies. If demands continued for new agencies to co-ordinate other work, then it was necessary to look at the old ones and consider killing off three for every new agency created.

IBM's managing director in the United Kingdom, Edward Nixon, who felt there was a need for new institutions, with the Scottish Development Agency having "teeth", power and resources, exampled the present confusion problems facing a potential overseas investor in Scotland.

"If he were interested in oil or oil supporting services he would go to Aberdeen and probably find himself talking to an organisation called the North East of Scotland Development Association. It has a staff of about 18 and no budget – a loose organisation of local authorities. The people are very helpful, give a lot of information, but are not really too significant from his point of view."

At Inverness is the Highlands and Islands Development Board, which has a staff of 200, several millions of pounds, but according to Nixon "it is really interested in keeping the crofts alive" (Rear Admiral David Dunbar-Nasmith, vice chairman of the HIDB pointed out that the organisation's approach to economic development was across the board, with industry fitted in which was appropriate to the size of the population. Investment created, both public and private over the past nine years, was significant in relation to the population of the area). In Edinburgh the potential investor would find the Scottish Office and the Scottish Council (Development and Industry). And finally in London he would come across the Department of Trade and Industry.

Support for the Scottish Development Agency was fairly widespread.

The former Permanent Under-Secretary of State at the Scottish Office, Sir Douglas Haddow, now chairman of the North of Scotland Hydro-Electric Board, was in agreement with Mackie about not creating an increasing number of agencies.

With almost startling frankness the ex-head of the Civil Service in Scotland admitted:

"The only reason I ever found for proliferating agencies was that it gave politicians an impression that they were doing something."

He wanted to see the Scottish Development Agency incorporate at least the Scottish Industrial Development Office (part of the Department of Trade and Industry), the Offshore Supplies Office (part of the Department of Energy), the Highlands and Islands Development Board, and the six Scottish new town development corporations.

Shipbuilder Sir William Lithgow was in favour of an SDA if it was free from the centralist restraints which people in Scotland had demonstrated clearly they would not accept. He complained that industry was constantly being told that "Auntie knows best" but that there were too many "Aunties" in distant places, and even small companies had to go to Brussels, where the EEC headquarters are, to find out some of the facts about agencies which were set up supposedly to assist industry. And a former Minister of State for Scotland in the 1971–74 Conservative Government, Lord Polwarth, thought that the setting up of the SDA, properly conceived with proper functions, was a step forward in the devolutionary process which was taking place in government.

Professor Alexander was interested, too, in the form of the Scottish Development Agency. He wanted the emphasis placed on industrially-oriented investment, with the agency concerned about injecting new ideas, stimulating and restructuring industry, and associating itself with the physical planning powers of the Scottish Secretary and the work of the Manpower Commission in training and the Department of Employment in manpower policy generally.

"Only then do we get what I think we need," he said. "A body capable of producing a development strategy for Scotland.

If one thinks of such an agency then the character of its staff, its board members and the executive becomes very clear. They must be people with industrial experience, managers and trades unionists, people with experience of commerce, and of the financial world, rather different from either politicians or civil servants. They must be people who will be able to make judgments in the areas of industrial development."

The support for a Scottish Development Agency and the other matters contained in the Scottish TUC policy statement were, according to Boyd, symptomatic of the general attitude of the organised British worker towards directing the nation's efforts to benefit the community.

Boyd, himself, at the Trades Union Congress in September 1974 had moved the following:

Congress calls on the Government to institute an urgent full scale inquiry into the energy needs and resources of Britain during the next ten years.

In addition, Congress believes that some form of Standing Commission with full participation from unions involved in the fuel and power industries is required to review and up-date the findings of the inquiry.

Congress further suggests that such an inquiry should take the following points into consideration:

1. The need for co-ordination of all forms of energy supply
2. an examination of manufacturing industries normally associated with oil and coal
3. the fullest possible development of the British coal industry
4. a full investigation into the many ways of economising on scarce fuel resources in both home and industry
5. the use of government machinery to investigate and control the domestic and international activities of the giant multi-national oil companies
6. the expansion of research and development of the nuclear programme
7. the need to pursue a co-ordinated investment and pricing policy by the Gas Corporation and other nationalised industries to ensure that the rate of exploitation of gas and oil resources is not inconsistent with the need to conserve those resources in the national interest.

Congress declares full support for the nationalisation of natural resources and to this end calls for the public ownership of North Sea oil and gas to bring this important source of energy under the complete control of Parliament and the people.

Congress also endorses the Government's action in declaring itself in favour of the purchase and development of British equipment and technology in the field of nuclear energy.

Earlier in the year the government-sponsored National Economic Development Council published a study of the impact of higher energy costs on British Industry[1]. The report examined nearly 50 industries which accounted for over 80% of the manufacturing output and around 60% of the gross domestic product. The report examined, over a three year period, the impact of higher energy prices, not only on the direct costs of industry but also on demand prospects. Industries most likely to be affected by direct cost increases were chemicals, fertilisers, inland transport, cement and building materials. Higher transport costs would lead to a greater use of larger vehicles with high load factors. Cement and bricks were estimated to rise in price between 35–50% and 20–25% respectively.

In certain areas, dearer primary energy would sharply reduce consumer demand which would obviously affect production industries concerned. The most severely affected in that respect were likely to be motor manufacture and other consumer durables, such as electronic appliances and clothing. It was estimated that petrol price increases alone would increase the running costs of a private motor car by 40% between 1973 and 1977 and the Report anticipated a shift towards smaller cars. Generally, the Report painted a gloomy picture of living standards over the next few years as a result of energy price increases.

Manpower

Two hundred years ago Dr Samuel Johnson said about agricultural Scotland:

1 *Energy: The increased cost of energy – Implications for U.K. Industry:* NEDO: H.M.S.O., 1974.

"Until Scotland can keep more of its natural leaders the Scottish economy will continue to suffer."

Effective manpower planning, stated Boyd, was a priority issue requiring integration between industry and the community. The example of Europe should be looked at and a study made of the Swedish Labour Market Board (See Appendix 2) which was entrusted with the application of regional development policies as well as manpower policies. The Labour Market Board has a budget equivalent of 15% of the total national income or 5% of central government expenditure. It has been considered highly successful in training and redeployment.

Throughout most of Europe, day-release for further education was compulsory for young people and it was time this was agreed on throughout the United Kingdom. At the present time, only a very small proportion of young people go on day or block-release for further education. The figures for October 1973 supplied by the Scottish Office were 9,383 girls and 49,766 boys, a total of 59,149 attending such courses.

A rise in the number of craft apprentices and technical trainees was needed to provide the skills required at the present time which would allow for adaptability in the future. It involved joint responsibility of industry, trades unions, and government. The Industrial Training Boards and industry, if used properly, could provide the skills and much of the manpower research forecasting (if given the funds).

Ten Government Training Centres were strategically situated giving training in skills for 25 trades – but not of craft standard. The type of centre could be expanded to bridge the gap in providing labour where shortages might exist, particularly the areas where rapid development was due to North Sea oil and gas discoveries. Despite the rich prospects, if critical shortages grew and make-shift planning was used to provide short-term solutions, those regions could become disaster areas in the long-term.

One of the problems to be faced was how to assure that the

right skills and abilities were available in the areas where they were needed most.

"The research we engage in, the ability to make raw materials into goods which are in demand, suffers because the 'sack' is still looked upon as the 'sack' and if anybody is sacked then the call is for defensive action immediately on the part of the trade union movement. It is no credit that, as one of the oldest manufacturing nations in the world which can face any challenge depending on skills and ingenuity, when the demands of the markets cause one firm to find itself not needing X number of workers, despite the fact that another firm could do with them, they are declared redundant."

He urged that the word "sack" should be dropped from the English vocabulary and job-change and re-training should receive attention.

Donald McCallum, director and general manager of Ferranti's in Scotland was in agreement. His point – re-training is a major issue. If money was to be spent on research, it had to produce change and that meant changes in jobs, which in turn meant an attitude of mind that the "sack" was not necessarily a bad thing, but an opportunity. To use the opportunities, however, it was necessary to re-train people.

Lord Polwarth, thought that training was essential to create conditions in which highly-advanced industries could be profitable. It was necessary to upgrade the labour resources all round, at managerial, technological and other levels. One of the most important and enormous tasks to be tackled was on the training front, by putting vastly more resources from government and industry into equipping labour to meet the demands of the highly technological industries seeking to make profits – and ensuring that those profits were made in Scotland. It had been an area thoroughly neglected, not so much by industry, but by successive governments. Polwarth also wanted a large amount of money made available to the trade union movement to assist it with the task of increasing resources in the field of education, to put it on par with the German trade union movement, so that the economic facts of life could be better understood by members of trades unions.

Boyd thought that the realm of adult education was important too. He referred to the Russell Report,[2] which was published in 1974, but applied only to England and Wales. Since then, however, the Alexander Report on adult education is due to be published in Scotland.

The Committee on adult education under the chairmanship of Professor Kenneth Alexander was appointed in May 1970 with the terms of reference:

"To consider the aims appropriate to voluntary leisure time courses for adults which are educational but not specifically vocations; to examine the extent to which these are being achieved at present; and with due regard to the need to use available resources most effectively, to make recommendations."

The report was sent to the Secretary of State for Scotland in December 1974 with over sixty recommendations.

Two of the recommendations of the Committee are similar to the points put forward by Polwarth. One puts forward the view that the teaching institutions and the trades unions should co-operate in securing an expansion of shop steward training, with greater use made of the Trades Union Congress Education Service as a point of contact between them in planning and content of courses. The other is that the Government through the Scottish Education Department should explore, in consultation with other interested parties, the possibility of establishing a residential college and regional centre for industrial relations training. (One of the organisations with which the Committee consulted was the Scottish International Education Trust. Alexander had a previous connection with two of the Trustees, Sir Iain Stewart and chairman James Houston, when all three were involved as directors of Fairfield (Glasgow) Ltd, which with Government, private

2 *Adult Education: A Plan for Development:* H.M.S.O., 1973.

and trade union funds had moved in to take over the Fairfield Shipbuilding and Engineering Company, in Glasgow, which had gone into liquidation in 1965, to create a new situation in industrial relations in shipbuilding. SIET in 1971, with Glenrothes Technical College, attempted to set up an industrial relations unit for management and trade unions. It failed mainly because of lack of management support. In 1973, however, SIET contributed £1,500 for a four day seminar at St Andrew's University on industrial relations, at which a large number of participants to the Glenrothes experiment attended).

Among the main recommendations of the Committee are that adult education should be regarded as an aspect of community education and with the youth and community service, should be incorporated into a community education service. The aim is to double the number of students by the mid 1980s and that the Secretary of State for Scotland should from time to time invite the education authorities to inform him of their plans for development along agreed lines. High priority in the deployment of resources has to be given to the needs of areas of multiple deprivation.

It is suggested that a new scheme of grants be instituted by the Secretary of State for Scotland with the object of enabling approved associations to initiate developmental programmes. And the arrangements for grants under the Further Education (Scotland) Regulations 1959 to approved associations engaged in adult education towards their administration costs should be continued.

The Workers' Educational Association, which should concentrate its efforts on promoting the educational needs of the socially, economically and educationally disadvantaged and be assisted by the education authorities, would continue to be regarded as eligible for such grants and the extra-mural departments of the universities should be recognised as approved associations for the purpose. M. T. Sweeney, regional education officer of TUC, Glasgow dissented from the recommendations about the Workers' Educational Association.

Among other recommendations: education authorities should be required to compile and maintain, in co-operation with social work departments and other appropriate organisations a register of all handicapped persons in their areas in order to establish their educational needs and ensure that these are met; provision increased for a wide range of Scottish traditional and cultural subjects; the use of Gaelic in Gaelic speaking areas for some subjects in adult programmes; the setting up of a fourth TV channel based on the BBC, which would not be devoted exclusively to education programmes; two new national bodies for the administration of educational broadcasting, one with executive functions to determine educational programme policy and the allocation of programme time, and the other with "watchdog" functions.

Boyd wanted to see paid educational leave for workers (a recommendation in the Russell Report, but not in the Alexander Report). France and Germany were two European countries committed to such a policy through legislation, with France having the most comprehensive plan, where workers were given extensive paid leave to improve their qualifications or educational attainments – a recognition of the rapidly changing society. The International Labour Organisation had adopted paid leave for educational purposes as a "Social Right".

The Manpower Services Commission which had been established in Britain still needed to have the resources to expand training and to greatly increase the training opportunities available to those who had lost their jobs through technological change and declining industries. Planning to avoid peaks and troughs in employment which had risen from shortsighted industrial planning was urgently required.

"Investment in human welfare means feeding the minds as well as the body", maintained Boyd. "Our education systems, our training schemes, our technical colleges and universities are all known for their high standard. They will be able to add to our growing requirements. Scotland, especially as the opportunities grow, must be prepared to provide adequate numbers of properly trained and educated men and women. Only in that way will the Scots be prepared to meet this new and challenging era."

(In the "feeding of minds" Boyd did not make any reference to the part the Arts might play, but Alex Dunbar, director of the Scottish Arts Council brought up the subject of the quality of life as opposed to the quantity of jobs. Government and local government were rightly concerned with essential services such as employment and housing, education, communications, and the environment, but public expenditure on these items only made sense if a fraction was invested in the arts, entertainment, recreation and sport. According to the Government Paper *Public Expenditure to 1977–78* the largest percentage change, 52%, in spending in Scotland over the next few years is on the Arts. But as Dunbar pointed out, it was only an increase from a "pittance" of £3.3 million in 1972–73 to a "pittance" of £5 million in 1977–78. The economic needs of the Arts, however, were extremely great, the effect of inflation had been catastrophic and would continue to be so because of the economic nature of the performing arts – they are unable to increase productivity. Nicholas Fairbairn Q.C. now M.P. for Kinross and West Perthshire made a similar point at the 1973 International Forum.)

Like others at the Forum, Boyd felt that manpower resources are the essential key to Scotland's growth and prosperity, with labour as the greatest asset, whatever the implications of North Sea discoveries.

And one aspect of manpower investment which he considered important was the work which has been started by the Health and Safety Commission set up on October 1, 1974, to create, improve and operate systems of regulations and codes of practice.

The Health and Safety Commission was set up two and a half years after the Committee of Inquiry on Safety and Health at Work,[1] headed by Lord Robens, had reported to Maurice

1 Safety and Health at Work, 1970–1972: H.M.S.O.

Macmillan, the Employment Minister in the Conservative Government. The Committee had been appointed in May 1970 by Barbara Castle, the then Secretary of State for Employment and Industry in the Labour Government.

Among the findings were the rather startling statistics that in Britain about 1,000 people a year were killed at their work, with a further 500,000 injured. At that time – and the figures have not diminished to any great extent – 23 million working days were lost in Britain each year through industrial injury and disease.

The Committee of Inquiry recommended the reform of the traditional approach to safety and health at work based on an ever-increasing, detailed statutory regulations which was outdated, over-complex and inadequate. The aim should be to create the conditions of more effective self-regulation by employers and workpeople jointly. Encouragement had to be given to the efforts of industry and commerce to tackle their own safety and health problems, supported and supplemented by up-to-date provisions unified within a single, comprehensive framework of legislation, with a much greater use of agreed voluntary standards and codes of practice to promote progressively better conditions. The broader and more flexible framework would enable the statutory inspection services to be used more constructively in advising and assisting employers and workpeople, and at the same time it would enable them to be concentrating more effectively on serious problems where tighter monitoring and control were needed.

Scotland's Money

"Investors and their advisers may consider that they have the right to do what they like with what is their own, but I would sincerely hope that everyone would accept the disciplines that responsible citizenship demands. Money must be channelled into investment sources which create real wealth in the form of goods and services, which not only improve the standard of living of the nations, but also assist in enriching the quality of the life of its people. As I see it, if privileged to be a private investor, there is a responsibility towards the community as a whole."

It is a view with which few investment managers would agree.

Boyd, however, argued that though the Scots had been pioneers in many forms of finance – investment trusts, branch banking, insurance, and unit trusts – with dynamic Scottish institutions performing an important part in developing Scotland in the nineteenth century, over the past years Scottish financiers had used the greater part of their resources for investing outside Scotland, where they considered there were far better opportunities for a high return on their assets. *While their enterprise benefitted Scottish investors it was a great loss to Scotland.* The unwillingness of Scottish financiers to invest in Scotland had been understandable, but it had helped to produce a vicious circle in which the lack of capital investment led to a decline in industrial opportunities, which further discouraged investment.

In the present day, the Scottish institutions were as efficient as ever and he hoped that North Sea oil and other important Scottish ventures would re-cycle mass Scottish finance back into the economy. There was substantial evidence, that it was beginning to take place. In the banking sector, for example, Scotland's largest bank, the Royal Bank of Scotland which along with Williams, Glyn made up the National and Commercial Banking Group, estimated that it had over £90 million directly tied up in the North Sea oil industry and a great deal more indirectly involved. It was trying to offer customers a package deal and had set up a Corporate Finance Department specifically for this purpose. The Bank of Scotland and Barclays Bank had each subscribed for 15% of the equity of the International Energy Bank, a new consortium of banks which is prepared to finance projects worth as much as £1,000 million.

Scotland had considerable financial resources – the investment trusts have combined assets worth about £2,000 million, Scottish insurance control assets of around £2,700 and the banks at least £1,500. The outstanding balance of National

Savings over the past five years had been nearly £200 million.

The *Investors Chronicle* in its 1973 Scottish Survey had appraised that *investment managers* in Scotland were responsible for over *£3,500 million* on behalf of life insurance companies, investment trusts and unit trusts. "This takes into consideration that a proportion of these institutions' assets are under their financial jurisdiction for investing," said Boyd.

Such a criticism of the financial institutions was not left unanswered.

William Coats, a director of Coats Patons put on another hat – as director of a trust – to say that there seemed to be a feeling that the people who had the money i.e. the insurance companies, the pension funds, the investment trusts, had it on their own account. But that was not true. They were trustees for other people, for the policy holders, the pensioners – even though investment trusts were slightly different in the class of people they dealt with, a large number of the shareholders were small investors. The degree of risk that could be taken, therefore, was a good deal less than if it was their own money. One of the problems of the present day over risk and return for trustees, was that at the present time nearly 17% could come in perpetuity from the Government, but it would not be so in the future necessarily. So the 17% is taken.

Banker John Harley, regional general manager in the North of Scotland for the Royal Bank of Scotland, claimed that the banks were doing their best but had become the "whipping boys" because of limits imposed by Government.

More money for lending could not be raised by the banks because they were banned by the Government from increasing their interest-bearing deposits beyond certain limits. The banks also followed the code of not borrowing short and lending long, which had led to the accusation that the Scottish banks and English clearing banks were "fuddy duddies". But they were still in business while "fringe" banks involved in the opposite attitude were having problems. The Scottish banks, asserted Harley, were doing their best to support Scottish industry, particularly in the oil field.

Peter de Vink, a director of Ivory and Sime, an investment managing company, explained that just as job re-allocation was misunderstood by most people so too was the maximisation of return on investment. Money was like water, it would eventually find its own level. Basically, money power resources followed manpower resources and not the other way round.

Though Boyd accepted that the banks and institutions were restricted in the use of money, he thought the point was being over-emphasised.

"If my money goes into the bank I will not be asked my opinion as to where the bankers will invest it. I don't expect them to. Of course the institutions are restricted but it doesn't stop them from giving leadership."

Author's note: On January 31st, 1975, a consultative document on the role of the Scottish Development Agency was issued by the Government. The functions which the Government envisaged the SDA would have included: acting as an investment bank to Scottish industry, providing loan finance and equity (the SDA would have an initial £200 million); having joint commercial ventures with private companies, and launching new ventures to create employment; giving managerial/financial advice to industry; promoting new investment in Scotland; the clearing and rehabilitation of derelict land and creating new major redevelopment schemes; environmental regeneration of urban or semi-urban areas.

The Agency would have a governing board, appointed by the Scottish Secretary of State who would determine policy, and a staff structure headed by a chief executive. The statutory powers and responsibilities of the Agency will extend to the whole of Scotland, though the responsibilities of the Highlands and Islands Board will remain unchanged. The SDA would take over the functions of the Scottish Industrial Estates Management Corporation which is responsible for the running of Government factories.

The SDA is expected to start operating by December 1975.

chapter 10

Conclusions

One of the subjects discussed at the International Forum was "thinking agencies" – the need to have in Scotland a creative and innovative research organisation. The Scottish Council, as was stated, is going ahead with a plan to outline a research policy for Scotland. In doing so they will have discussions with various organisations, universities and the Government. They could do worse than hold similar forums, even mini-versions, every three or six months merely to extract, if nothing else, the various ideas produced during the "hothouse" atmosphere created by such a gathering. Collecting such a group of people at Aviemore, three hours away from the nearest Scottish city, five hours from London, practically ensures the undivided attention of all taking part – miles away from office desks, factories or university lecture-rooms. They are all there – the businessmen and the academics, the economists and the trades unionists, the communicators and the clergy, the scientists and the politicians – with little to divert them, apart from the scenery. The cross-fertilisation of ideas and discussion goes on long after the formal sessions are over.

The Forum is a mind-stimulating event which has produced in its relatively short history, so far, some quite remarkable peaks of thought.

In 1972, for instance, Dutchman Jan de Vries staggered the participants with a mind-bending paper on energy and his views about the possible use of hydrogen power in the future.

As was stated in Chapter 7, Strathclyde University is becoming involved with a small part of the world-wide research into the subject. It has taken just over two years for it to happen, but it was stimulated by the remarks made by de Vries. And might it just not be possible that the forceful discussion at the 1973 Forum about the need for the Scottish Office to take into its authority industrial development in Scotland – said during the period of a Conservative Government – helped to bring about that very thing? On July 1, 1975 the present Secretary of State for Scotland in a Labour Government has it under his jurisdiction. Let it be admitted quickly, however, that he has had such a move in mind for some time.

At the 1974 International Forum, the effect of Peter Odell's predictions on North Sea oil potential, from the work being done by him and his team at Rotterdam, were undoubtedly overwhelming. Whether they are correct or not is another question. But it would seem that it is time for a change in the official Government circle's attitude of "it's that fellow Odell again". The Forum might, indeed, be historic because of Odell's predictions. But will it be because in ten years time, having been ignored in the meantime, he will be proved right? Should not the Department of Energy, the Government, and the sceptics *now* show why Odell's figures are wrong – if they are wrong? Should they be correct, then the economic situation in Scotland would alter beyond all recognition, and the situation for Britain, and Western Europe, change dramatically during the current crisis. As the chief economic adviser to the Scottish Office, Gavin McCrone, said: "If Professor Odell is right and that we are all thinking too low, if he is right, then it changes the nature of so many of the things that we have to think about in Scotland . . . the gloom which many economists share about the short-term situation, the fact that owing to the higher energy prices many countries in Western Europe must be running with huge balance of payments deficits up to 1980, that situation and the worrying effect it has on the balance of payments and all the rest of it, though we cannot get out of it by the Odell route, *we can make a huge difference to it.* . . ."

McCrone, like Peter Jay, preferred the attitude of Professor MacKay of Aberdeen University, who spoke at the British Association conference at Stirling in the autumn of 1974.

The quotation is worthy of another mention to illustrate a point –

"The *guesses* (the italics are added) I have put forward would suggest that the North Sea oil activities might lead directly to the creation of some 25,000–30,000 additional jobs. The employment will be highly concentrated and will transform the economic prospects of certain areas . . . however, these lie outside the industrial heartland of the country, and in particular are removed from the Clydeside area, which is the focus of the greatest social and economic problems. It is therefore quite possible that the direct impact from North Sea oil will still leave Clydeside, and hence the Scottish economy as a whole, with the familiar problems of low incomes, high unemployment and high emigration . . . my own view would be that the direct impact of North Sea oil and gas offers too narrow and restricted an industrial base to transform the prospects for the whole of the Scottish economy . . ."

On January 10, 1975 Minister of State Bruce Millan announced that the Scottish Office had given permission for three sites on the Clyde to be used for the building of concrete platforms for the North Sea. The investment by the firms would be hundreds of millions of pounds, and 1500 permanent jobs will be available. The prediction was that the Clyde will become the largest oil platform construction centre in Europe.

Odell's "closed system" theory – keeping oil in the North Sea for Europe's needs – would require a collective political decision, and his thoughts of a European oil bank, to which the 250 million people of the EEC could subscribe £1 each and thereby raise some cash for oil developments could be dismissed as riding a hobby horse. But his sums cannot be taken so lightly – nor should they be. What would be the impact if his "guess" is right?

His views certainly made an impact on the participants at the Forum, even if, like so many others in the country, they are still confused about just how big North Sea oil is likely to be.

Jay's view about a payroll subsidy, if not as dramatic as Odell's contribution was, nevertheless, thought-provoking and should warrant some examination in official circles, if it has not already done so. In the present inflationary crisis, which all agree will continue for some years ahead, new thinking is required after the failure of the well-worn "stop-go" policies of the past fourteen years; policies which affected Scotland much more deeply than most other parts of the country. As Scottish TUC general secretary James Jack was wont to remark, and it was echoed in other places by Hamish Grant, Scottish secretary of the Confederation of British Industry, "Scotland never did suffer from its economy over-heating". Investment grants and loans to induce industry into Scotland, though not entirely unsuccessful, do not now seem to have the attraction for, or the influence on, industry which some consider they have. Perhaps a new approach is necessary. (Jay's reference to a separate Scottish currency was more serious than most of the participants realised).

John Boyd remarked that over the years in Scotland and the United Kingdom there had been a tendency to wait until an adverse situation arose before attempting to rectify it. This had led to patching and repair work instead of getting to the root of the problem. And he quoted the *Financial Times* which had said: "Scotland's institutional representatives – those of industry and finance houses, among its trade unions and development agencies and within Government – have become conditioned by the need to seek ways out of economic difficulties rather than ways into economic opportunities."

Odell and Jay might well have pointed the way towards a change in fundamental thinking.

Boyd raised another issue which needs re-thinking. A problem which many people have applied their minds to, some have attempted to solve, governments have "tinkered with", and trades unions have been to some extent hypocritical about. Effective manpower planning (and all that means in re-training, job alternatives for the redundant, reorganisation of employment due to technological changes).

It was the one investment on which everyone was agreed – industrialists like shipbuilder Sir William Lithgow, whose company finds itself in the position of being able to offer hundreds of jobs but is in an area of high unemployment; academics like Professor Kenneth Alexander who has been deeply involved in the subject for many years, both in his capacity as professor of economics at Strathclyde University and someone who is involved in industry – he is chairman of Govan Shipbuilders in Glasgow; and the politicians in the form of Bruce Millan, the spokesman for the Government.

Millan admitted that he did not think any government had got to grips with the very serious manpower problems.

"I think it is a neglected area not only in Scotland but in the U.K. and I hope that the new Manpower Service Commission and the new Training Services Agency will be able to help in this area."

It is a subject which the new Scottish Development Agency, when it is formed, may consider as a matter of priority, because not only is it a matter of "investment" but an issue which is fundamental to the problem of industrial relations.

Opinions on investment in research were sharply divided. There were those who wanted more research done in Scotland on "something", even if they were not quite sure what that something should be. Others took the view that research is being done both in Scotland and elsewhere in the world and that to increase the amount was not a "good" investment. The Scottish Council's decision to go ahead with a plan to outline a research policy for Scotland would identify those areas which might produce important results.

Perhaps, as a start, a Scottish "think tank" might consider the three fundamental issues raised at the International Forum – forward thinking on the effects of North Sea oil, changes in the pattern of Government assistance for industry, a new approach to manpower.

Such an *investment* might be the best of all – not only for Scotland, but for Britain as a whole.

appendix 1

Pattern of Public Expenditure in Scotland — Extract

Prepared by Scottish Council Research Institute

The Scottish Council Research Institute produced a report of a study made for International Forum. The complete report is, in itself, too long to produce in full. The most significant tables have been extracted to provide information which will lead to a possible better understanding on the chapters "Public Investment" and "Private Investment". The complete report is available through International Forum, Scottish Council (Development and Industry), 33 Castle Street, Edinburgh.

Table I shows the main items of public expenditure on trade and industry for which figures of Scottish expenditure are available, or for which reasonable estimates can be made. The principal omission is current account financial support for the nationalised industries. Total British expenditure under this heading, including transport industries, amounted to £312 million in 1972/3 and £711 million in 1973/4. It is not possible to disaggregate these figures regionally, but it is probable that the share attributable to Scotland would be roughly proportional to the share of nationalised industries' capital expenditure (and operating activities). Much of the current financial support would be attributable to a general shortfall between the prices and costs of nationalised industries. Differential elements e.g. subsidies to transport operations in the Highlands and Islands, and to British Rail commuter services in the South-East, may tend to balance.

Table 1 Public Expenditure on Trade, Industry and Employment

£ million	1972/3			1964/5–1972/3		
Private Industry	Scotland	G.B.	Scotland %	Scotland	G.B.	Scotland %
Investment grants	34·6	295	11·7	326·4	2,565	12·7
Selective, Regional and General Assistance	3·1	18	17·2	3·1	18	17·2
Local Employment Act	26·2	69	38·0	165·8	528	31·4
REP and SET (additional payments)	37·2	101	36·8	248·0	811	30·6
Shipbuilding Industry	(29·5)	81	36·4	(44·0)	148	29·7
Employment Services and Redundancy Fund	21·7	200	10·9	79·6	942	8·5
Aircraft+Aerospace projects		(126)			(729)	
National Space Programme		(4)			(78)	
General R & D Support	(10·0)	(5)	8·1	(55·0)	(108)	5·1
Other Assistance (incl. films, tourism IRC, General investment, cotton)		(—11)			(157)	
Refinancing Export Credit	(30·0)	297	10·1	(30·0)	297	10·1
total	192·3	1,185	16·2	951·9	6,381	14·9

Nationalised Industries Capital Expenditure

	Scotland	G.B.	Scotland %	Scotland	G.B.	Scotland %
Fuel and Power	113·1	689	16·4	486·7	3,669	13·3
Steel	(15·0)	190	7·9	(73·0)	766	9·5
Post Office	54·1	635	8·5	199·6	2,367	8·4
Airways and airports	0·7	73	1·0	2·0	458	0·4
Surface Transport	19·6	96	20·4	67·3	528	12·7
total	202·5	1,683	12·0	828·6	7,788	10·6

Sources: Scottish Abstract Statistics 1973.
National Income and Expenditure 1973.
Trade and Industry – various issues.
Industry Act 19.2: Annual Report 1972/3.
West Central Scotland Plan.

( ) = Estimate

One of the most striking features shown by the analysis is the very high proportion of total public expenditure on industry taken by the nationalised industries. Including current support, the nationalised industries accounted for almost £2,000 million or 63% of a total expenditure of £3,180 million in 1972/3. These figures are relevant in the context of a discussion of what could, or should, be the "targets" for increasing the proportion of public expenditure spent in Scotland. While a good deal of public expenditure on the nationalised industries is severely constrained in terms of geographical location, e.g. provision of electricity capacity, there are substantial elements for which locationary discretion is possible. The provision of steel plant, certain sectors of the energy and telecommunications industries, airport and port facilities, and headquarters and R & D operations across the board are all, to a greater or lesser extent, discretionary in terms of location choice. Total capital expenditure on the nationalised industries in Scotland over the past nine years has been, at 10.6% of the British total, only marginally higher than the Scottish share of population (9.6%). While this is only a very crude measure of differential expenditure, there are clear and important potential investment opportunities in Scotland in the nationalised industries which would increase this proportion.

Within the total of public expenditure on private industry, only a relatively low proportion comes from policies specifically directed towards regional development. Allowing for the regional differential element within the investment grants total, regional policy expenditure amounted to approximately £245 million in 1972/3; 29% of total public expenditure on private industry, or 8% of public expenditure on all industries, including the nationalised sector. Thus while Scotland receives more than one third of total regional policy expenditure, its share of total public expenditure on private industry is very much less. From aid to private industry, other than regional policy measures, Scotland does well in terms of shipbuilding expenditure, but relatively poorly from aid to the aerospace industry; while some very large expenditure items, such as employment services and refinancing of export credit, are disbursed more or less equally between all regions of Britain.

Agriculture, fishing, forestry

Scotland receives a substantial proportion of total British public expenditure in all these sectors, but almost all of it is directly related to her share of production in these industries. Very little of the spending represents special assistance over and above the financial support received by comparable sectors elsewhere in Britain.

Table 2 Public Expenditure on Agriculture, Fishing and Forestry

£ million	Scotland 1972/3	G.B. 1972/3	Scotland %	Scotland 1964/5– 1972/3	G.B. 1964/5– 1972/3	Scotland %
Agriculture Support	49·5	254	19·5	416·9	2,401	17·4
Other Agriculture Assistance	16·8	121	13·9	80·1	523	15·3
Fishing	5·7	12	47·5	32·4	62	52·3
Forestry	21·3	51	41·8	143·4	344	41·7
total	93·3	438	21·3	672·8	3,330	20·2

In the year 1972/3 Scotland accounted for 14% of the agricultural area of Britain (excluding rough grazing) and for 12% of the gross value of agricultural production. There are two main reasons why Scotland's share of public expenditure on agriculture in that year was significantly above these levels. Firstly, the composition of Scottish agricultural output is weighted towards those products on which financial support is relatively high, particularly livestock.

The second reason for the high share of total expenditure is the fact that Scotland receives a very high proportion of current account grants to Special Areas, which are virtually all associated with raising sheep and cattle in hill-farming areas.

The other major recent change in public spending on agriculture has been the very large extension of food subsidies in 1974, some paid direct to farmers and some to consumers.

These are currently running at an annual rate of £500 million, possibly rising to £700 million next year. Because these are overwhelmingly concentrated on milk and dairy products (nearly 80% of the total), in which Scotland is relatively weak, Scottish agriculture receives relatively less than other regions of Britain.

Two expenditure priorities may be highlighted for Scottish agriculture, one short-term and one long-term. There is no doubt that there is an immediate and serious problem for livestock farmers in Britain, squeezed between massive cost increases for fuel and feed and declining market prices. The problem is especially marked for Scotland, because of the high concentration on livestock production, and government financial aid is urgently needed to alleviate farmers' losses and to forestall the future meat shortages which will arise if the current rage of slaughtering and non-replacement of stock continues.

The long-term expenditure priority is an increase in capital grants for improvement and modernisation, particularly in relation to marginal land. There is little doubt that substantial acreages of both low-lying and rough grazing could be made more productive by draining, fertilising, and improving management, if greater capital incentives were available. Under present Common Agricultural Policy (CAP) it seems unlikely that the amount of such grants to Scottish farmers will be substantially increased. Under the original Mansholt plan for the modernisation of European agriculture by 1980, one-third of total EEC expenditure on agriculture was to go on farm improvement. This plan is now forgotten and currently only about one-tenth of CAP expenditure goes in farm investment grants. Whatever the direct economic return to be expected from such capital grants, there is one major indirect benefit from capital grants designed to increase agricultural production in Scotland. Britain still imports nearly half of her food supplies, and imports of indigenous-type products account for approximately 27% of the total value of food consumed, at a cost of well over £1,000 million per annum. Increased agricultural production represents one of the few sectors directly susceptible to import-substitution and consequent relief to the balance-of-payments deficit. While this consideration has been important in the past it is now, in the wake of the oil crisis and primary commodity price upsurge, a dominant economic consideration.

The volume of public expenditure on fishing is relatively small and stable, relating mainly to grants and loans for new vessels and equipment, harbour improvements, and research and development. The substantial Scottish share of such expenditure (47.5% in 1972/3) reflects closely her proportion of the British fishing fleet (45%) and tonnage of landings (46%).

One of the most interesting recent developments in the fishing industry is the growth of government and commercial activity in fish-farming. The Scottish coast offers excellent opportunities for fish farming, and nearly all British research is being conducted in Scotland, under the aegis of the White Fish Authority and the Highlands and Islands Development Board, including assistance to commercial concerns by the latter. The results of recent research are promising, and with sea-caught fish likely to become increasingly scarce and expensive, fish-farming could well become a major source of production in the near future. However, while government financial support is still required to support research, it seems likely that commercial prospects will increasingly be good enough to permit extension of production without large-scale public expenditure.

In 1972/3 Scotland received 42% of all public expenditure on forestry, the great bulk of which represented assistance to the Forestry Commission. This compares with a Scottish share of 53% of Forestry Commission acreage, and approximately 75% of all current new planting. The relatively low share of public spending is largely explicable in terms of grants to private landowners, a higher proportion of which go to England and Wales; and central administrative expenses, which will in future largely be concentrated in Scotland, with the moving of Forestry Commission head offices to Edinburgh.

The main area of discretion in future public expenditure is the rate of planting. Present plans, deriving from the 1972

197

policy statement on foresty which set the industry a target rate of 3% return (including defined social benefits) on its national capital, are for a very slow rate of expansion. The forestry area in Scotland would grow, at best, from the present 2 million acres to 3.5 million acres by the year 2000, and this would represent little improvement on the U.K.'s present 8% self-sufficiency in timber. The Scottish Council[1] has suggested that with an accelerated rate of planting, mostly in Scotland, Britain could become 25% self-sufficient within 50 years. The 1972 "Forestry Policy" guidelines have been criticised in the past for taking a narrow view of social benefits and of indirect economic effects in the stimulation of wood-processing jobs in areas with serious job needs. Since then, the world-wide shortage of timber and consequent high prices have been greatly exacerbated; and the potential balance-of-payments gain, albeit slow in developing, has added to the case for an accelerated rate of expenditure on planting.

Transport

Public expenditure on roads has been slightly higher than in the rest of Great Britain. This has applied equally to maintenance costs, and investment in new roads. But whereas total expenditure in Scotland has on average been about 11% of that in G.B., Scotland has over 13% of the total road mileage, and over 20% of trunk and principal roads (including motorways). This however must reflect the long distances between places throughout most of Scotland, more than the standard of provision in relation to demand. Although motorway construction began relatively late in Scotland, it has more than caught up with the rest of the U.K. The bulk of the population of Scotland is confined to a relatively small area, and it is mainly within this area that motorways are required. The mileages of motorway required need not, therefore, be particularly high relative to the rest of the U.K., although considerably more provision of trunk and principal roads is necessary in areas of sparse population.

1 *A Future for Scotland.* Scottish Council (Development and Industry), October 1973.

Table 3   Public Expenditure on Transport

£ million	Scotland 1972/3	G.B. 1972/3	Scotland %	Scotland 1964/5– 1972/3	G.B. 1964/5– 1972/3	Scotland %
Roads and public lighting	104·0	957	10·9	616·9	5,744	10·7
Ports	6·2	46	13·5	38·1	250	15·2
Support to British Rail	12·2	70	17·4	55·7*	435*	12·8*
Other surface transport	7·7	178	4·3			
total	130·1	1,251	10·3	710·7	6,429	11·0

* 1970/1–1972/3 only

Scotland has enjoyed a relatively high rate of public investment in ports over the last ten years. The proportion of total public expenditure in Great Britain is substantially greater than the proportion of goods handled, although this has grown in recent years. Only two other major port regions in Great Britain had a faster growth in traffic between 1965 and 1971: Yorks and Humberside experienced a 67% growth rate, and Wales a 48% growth, while in Scotland the rate was 28%.

Expenditure on ports reached a peak in real terms in 1967 in the wake of the recommendations of the Rochdale Report. This backlog of investment has now been made up, and total expenditure in real terms is now back to the level of the early 1960s.

Over the ten years 1963 to 1972 Scotland suffered slightly more reductions in rail-route mileages open. In Scotland the mileage fell by 38% compared with 32% in G.B. Scotland also received over 17% of the support given to British Rail for unremunerative services. Over the same period, passengers fell by 20%, and freight traffic by 26%. This pattern was the same in both G.B. and Scotland, although the amount of iron and steel carried by rail in Scotland rose, in contrast to a decline in G.B., and revenues from freight traffic were only 6.5% of the total for G.B. The steep fall to 1972 can be explained in part by the effects of industrial action. For the future British Rail hope to improve their competitiveness with the roads by introducing fast inter-city links.

Over the ten years 1963 to 1972, employment on the railways was reduced by half, in an effort to improve productivity. In Great Britain as a whole this has helped to compensate for declines in traffic: receipts rose from £463 million in 1963 to £564 million in 1972, and receipts per employee from £1,113 to £2,576 (an increase of over 130%). In Scotland, however, receipts fell from £42.9 million to £40.3 million, and receipts per employee increased from £947 to only £1,823.

Housing

The level of total Government housing subsidies paid in Scotland is high relative to those paid in G.B. as a whole. This level of subsidy is determined by several factors, and in order to explain Scotland's high subsidy level, it is necessary to look at some of these factors in more detail.

Up until the 1972 Housing Finance Act brought in by the last Conservative Government, Government financial assistance was paid to all Local Authorities to enable them to build and subsequently let houses at below cost rents. These payments were given annually, usually for the duration of the loan made for the initial building costs, and were rated according to the cost of the loan repayments. Three main factors, therefore, determined the amount of Government financial assistance given. Firstly, the total number of local authority houses in Scotland; second, the proportion of newer houses (which would cost more to build and entail larger loans per unit); and thirdly, the proportion of high-rise buildings, where the cost per unit is higher than for low-rise buildings, and the loans larger per unit.

Scotland has a very much higher percentage of public-sector housing than has G.B.; Scotland has more high-rise housing than the rest of G.B., and a larger amount of newer public-sector housing than has G.B. These are the primary factors determining the higher level of Government housing subsidies

Table 4 Public Expenditure on Housing

£ million	Scotland 1972/3	G.B. 1972/3	Scotland %	Scotland 1964/5– 1972/3	G.B. 1964/5– 1972/3	Scotland %
Subsidies	94·8	466	20·3	605·2	2,340	25·8
Improvement grants	14·7	95	15·5	31·3	235	13·3
Investment	141·7	790	17·9	1,099·1	6,598	16·7
Other	8·2	95	8·6	35·5	716	5·0
total	259·5	1,446	17·9	1,771·1	9,889	17·9

in Scotland; there is, however, one more factor which should be looked at, and this is slum-clearance programmes.

Government financial help was given to Local Authorities to help with the demolition of dwellings which were considered to fall below the tolerable standard set by the Housing Scotland Act 1969. This help was to be continued under the new 1972 Housing Act (and will doubtless be implemented under any replacement Act) and the size of this problem has to a small degree affected the level of subsidy.

Public expenditure in the future will largely depend on two factors – the level of future subsidies and the amount of investment in housing in the future.

The size of future Government housing subsidies will depend on what happens to the last Conservative Government's 1972 Housing Finance Acts, which are at present being held in abeyance. It is generally believed that any future Housing Finance Act will broadly consist of the context of the old Tory Act.

One of the Act's proposals was to alter the existing subsidy system. These existing subsidies were to be phased out over a transitional period, and were to be replaced by subsidies to meet the greater part of the cost of a new rent rebate and allowance scheme, and by new subsidies to assist those authorities with continuing housing needs, who must incur heavy expenditure in the future. These new subsidies consisted of the following:

1. a housing expenditure subsidy to assist authorities whose costs are increasing rapidly;

2. a high-cost subsidy for authorities with high overall housing costs;

3. a slum-clearance subsidy giving direct financial help to those authorities which still have to close or demolish houses that do not meet the tolerable standard.

If this system is broadly carried out in the future, the total level of Government subsidies for housing is likely to be down from the level for previous years, with some local authorities, of course, receiving more financial help than others.

The subsidy level will also depend on the amount of new investment that will take place. A sizeable proportion of Local Authorities' current expenditure is loan repayment on capital borrowed for housebuilding. For example, in 1970, Glasgow Corporation's loan repayment amounted to 67% of total current expenditure. Future housebuilding programmes will therefore influence future current expenditure.

Public housebuilding programmes are directly affected by central and local government policy decisions relating to the standard of provision and its achievement, and decisions on the general control public expenditure.

Public sector housebuilding programmes depend on the following:

1. number of households
2. stock of houses of a given standard
3. policy on what is a "tolerable" standard
4. policy on improvement, rather than replacement
5. the availability of resources (both financial and physical)
6. policy on the split between public and private housing, and how each should be financed.

The only official housing forecast available at the moment is by the National Economic Development Office, based on 1971, which forecasts a continued fall in public housebuilding from 29,100 completions in 1971 to 16,000 in 1977. These estimates were based on 1971 population statistics; further figures have been released since then on the birth-rate and net emigration, and other information from various sources has since been collected. These considerations bring our estimate of total housing need to 248,000, or an average of 41,000 per annum.

It has already been mentioned that housing policy is in a period of transition. There has been a change in the public sector domination of housebuilding in Scotland in the 1960s, when large programmes were geared to re-development; although this will continue over the next 10 years or so, it is likely to be on a reduced scale. Other factors have contributed to the declining importance of the public sector; for example, increasing affluence and the availability of finance led to an increased demand for private housing; rising costs and concern about the social environment of housing have led to new policies designed to encourage the improvement of older houses. However, during the 1970s mortgage rates and construction costs had risen to a level which is pricing many people out of the private housing market.

These, together with other considerations, have led us to estimate that the output of public housing is likely to settle at a level of about 21,000 per annum to 1977. This figure should be compared with the average number of completions in the public sector over a period of 19 years. The average over the whole period was 23,100 (peak year 1954 – 35,300 completions; lowest year 1961 – 19,500). One would expect, therefore, that the level of investment will fall because of a higher emphasis on low-rise/low-cost building than that which was evident during the 1960s.

Other factors which will affect future spending include:
1. Improvement grants paid by Local Authorities from Central Government Funds, to help house owners with the costs involved in house improvement. Although at present this only forms a small part of the total housing bill, it is a growing part and is likely to continue to grow.

2. Other assistance from public funds may be given to owner-occupiers, to encourage more home ownership.

3. Further expansion of Housing Associations which have been growing fast over the last few years. Although houses built by Housing Associations in 1972 accounted for only 1% of total completions, this proportion is likely to grow in the future. (Housing Associations are financed by Central Government through the Housing Corporation and by Local Authorities who can grant up to 100% loans to the associations.)

Education

In terms of public expenditure on education Scotland seems, at first sight, to compare relatively well with other British regions, accounting for 11.1% of total spending 1972/3 compared to a 9.6% share of British population. However, a detailed analysis reveals that only part of this differential reflects higher standards of educational provision, and in some respects Scotland is significantly below average British standards.

Expenditure on universities is the category in which Scottish spending is relatively high, as a proportion of the British total. A substantial part of this differential is due to the fact that Scotland serves as a place of university education for many students resident in, and returning to, other regions of Britain. At the latest count, 24% of all students in Scottish universities were resident outside Scotland, while only 6% of Scottish residents were educated at universities outside Scotland. In net terms, therefore, just under 20% of Scottish university expenditure is incurred on behalf of non-Scottish residents.

However, Scottish students do enjoy a substantially higher level of provision of university education than the remainder of Britain.

Both for men and women, the proportions of Scottish school-leavers going on to university are much higher than the average for England and Wales – and are 40% higher than even the "best" English region. It is, perhaps, a natural corollary that the Scottish proportions for other forms of higher education

Table 5   Public Expenditure on Education

£ million	Scotland 1972/3	G.B. 1972/3	Scotland %	Scotland 1964/5– 1972/3	G.B. 1964/5– 1972/3	Scotland %
Schools (incl. meals, milk)	266·1	2,270	11·7	1,510·5	13,035	11·6
Further Education+Teacher training	61·4	608	10·1	357·4	3,569	10·0
Universities	71·5	489	14·6	403·9	2,882	14·0
Other Education expenditure	24·3	431	5·6	167·1	2,602	6·4
total	423·3	3,798	11·1	2,438·9	22,088	11·0

should be somewhat lower than for England and Wales, particularly in view of the greater number of "near-university" establishments outside Scotland. However, while the overall position for men seems satisfactory, with more school-leavers going on to some form of full-time higher education than the British average, this does not hold true for women. Despite the much higher proportion of Scottish girls going to university, the total receiving some form of further, full-time education was only 20.5% in 1971–72, compared to 24.3% in England and Wales.

Valid comparisons of the standards of school education between Scotland and the rest of Britain are made virtually impossible by the different educational systems.

One field of education in which Scotland does seem to be seriously deficient is in the provision of nursery schools. In 1972 only 8.4% of all Scottish children aged 2–4 attended public or private nursery schools, compared to 15.7% for Britain as a whole.

Regardless of the educational merits or otherwise of nursery schools, this does represent a serious constraint on the ability of women with small children being able to take full or part-time employment. While it is hard to separate cause and effect, the proportion of young married women who are economically active is significantly lower in Scotland than in Great Britain as a whole: 35.9% in the 25–34 years age category in 1971 compared to 38.4% in Great Britain. If the economically active proportion could be increased by 2½%, bringing Scotland up to the British average, by the provision of more nursery school places, this would add nearly 7,000 females to the Scottish work-force in this age category alone. The expansion of nursery school places is already one of the top priorities of the British educational spending programme, but the present inferior level of provisions suggests it should be doubly so in Scotland. The costs of expanding provision should be relatively small, with nursery schools currently accounting for only around £2 million per annum, out of a total expenditure on schools of £266 million in 1972/3.

Note: In education, as by so many other social and economic criteria, the Glasgow area is below national Scottish standards. By nearly every criteria, Glasgow fares worse than any other Scottish region, with the differential particularly bad for school-leaving qualifications. In any consideration of education expenditure priorities, an increase in spending on schools in the Glasgow area must rank very highly.

Table 6   Public Expenditure on Health and Personal Social Services

£ million	Scotland 1972/3	G.B. 1972/3	Scotland %	Scotland 1964/5– 1972/3	G.B. 1964/5– 1972/3	Scotland %
Hospitals	201·3	1,770	11·4	1,168·8	10,059	11·6
Family Practitioners	57·0	584	9·8	373·4	3,757	9·9
Other	73·4	715	10·3	356·6	4,096	8·7
total	331·7	3,069	10·8	1,898·8	17,912	10·6

Health and Personal Social Services

In general, Scotland has a better provision of hospital and health services than have England and Wales, with the exception of the number of dentists and ophthalmic opticians. Scotland is in a pariticularly good position with regards the number of staffed beds and the number of medical, dental, professional and technical hospital staff per 1,000 population, compared with England and Wales.

Projected Public Expenditure

Consideration of the future prospects for public expenditure in Scotland must start from the background of overall British economic prospects and public spending plans. The latest official British expenditure projections, presented in *Public Expenditure to 1977–78*,[1] contain detailed extrapolations of planned spending on each programme item. In table 7, below, the implications for Scottish public expenditure are shown. The 1977–78 figures have been calculated by applying the proportions of each principal expenditure item spent in Scotland in 1972–73 to the projected British totals for 1977–78, modified only by allowing for recent changes in REP expenditure.

Table 7   Projected Public Expenditure in Scotland to 1977-8

Expenditure Category	1972/3 £m	1977/8 £m	% change %
Agriculture, forestry, fishing	93·3	79	−15
Trade, industry, employment:			
—Regional policy	84·0	184	+119
—Other assistance to industry and employment services	108·3	42	−61
—Nationalised industries' capital expenditure	202·5	277	+37
Roads and Transport	130·1	177	+36
Housing	259·4	318	+23
Education	423·3	506	+20
Health and personal social services	331·7	402	+21
Environmental services	132·4	148	+12
Social Security	508·6	601	+18
Miscellaneous:			
—Research councils	10·4	11	+6
—Law and order	74·2	94	+27
—Arts	3·3	5	+52
—Common services	65·3	72	+10
total, above items	2,426·8	2,916	+20
Public expenditure in Scotland as percentage of British expenditure	11·4%	11·6%	

Note: The figure for research councils does not include £4·8 million of grants and grants in aid made by the Department of Agriculture and Fisheries to research institutes.

1 H.M.S.O., December 1973.

The projections contained in the table should not be regarded as realistic forecasts, either of the total level of expenditure or of relative changes in composition. The British projections on which they are based take account of foreseeable changes in spending plans. Therefore, items such as "Other assistance to industry", which consists largely of *ad hoc* financial support for nationalised and private industries, include only known claims on spending, with the result that projected total expenditure declines sharply – although the probabilities are that new claims will arise within the projection period. Secondly, they are already seriously out-dated because they are based on the policies of a former Government, and because they were prepared before the full implications of the rise in oil prices and other recent economic developments were known. However, the projections are useful as a yardstick against which possible changes can be measured, particularly in terms of the total increase in public expenditure.

appendix 2

Swedish Employment Policy

Western European countries have had a long-standing com-
mittment to full employment, though at the present time the
policy is under a severe challenge, with inflation rising sharply.
During the 1960s and early 1970s the British attitude was that
inflation could not be countered without higher levels of unemployment in Western Europe. From February 1974 and
again after the October election, 1974 a Labour Government
pledged itself to a policy of lower unemployment, but found
the situation difficult to contain because of inflation and the
effect it was having on industry, where closures were taking
place. Scotland, like other parts of Britain, saw some of the
larger companies having redundancies, or at best, a cut-back
to a three or four day working week.

In January 1975, Chancellor of the Exchequer Denis Healey
warned, because of Government concern about rising unemployment and inflation, that jobs would have to take priority
over wages. Workers, even in prosperous industries, would have
to agree to lower wage rises to safeguard the jobs of people
elsewhere. The fight over the next few years would be to protect
jobs.

"It is far better that more people should be in work, even if
that means accepting lower wages on average, than that those
lucky enough to keep their jobs should scoop the pool while
millions are living on the dole."

The Government which is totally against a statutory incomes policy has to find a solution of containing excessive wage demands.

Santosh Mukherjee in a PEP Broadsheet[1] *Making Labour Markets Work – A Comparison of the U.K. and Swedish Systems*, wrote:

"Increasing worries, on the part of governments, about rapid price increases have made them think about labour markets. But that thinking has been mainly about the demand side. This is most clearly visible in Britain, though governments of other Western European countries too have shared these premises. This has meant, again most clearly in Britain, the use of fiscal and monetary policy to create unemployment. At its core, this strategy has involved a false assumption about the behaviour of labour markets. An increase in unemployment, on that reasoning, implied an increase in labour supply. And that in turn, by that process of reasoning, has been expected to reduce the pressure for wage increases. But the conditions needed to enable these things to happen have not existed. Labour markets have shown themselves, in conditions of full employment to be very imperfect markets indeed. In fact, the basis of the strategic assumption that there is one labour market within a country, open to manipulation by fiscal and monetary pressures, has proved false. If there had been a reasonable theory about labour markets, this kind of error could have been avoided. In the event, what has been demonstrated is the existence of a variety of sub-markets for labour, and many of these are rigged. Given that, it is wholly unsurprising that deflationary policies have had varying impacts on these sub-markets. The labour market as a whole has failed to respond to the prodding of overall, general deflationary policies. This is where the Swedes have contributed something new. They have recognised and taken as a basis for

1 Making Labour Markets Work: A Comparison of the U.K. and Swedish Systems: Santosh Mukherjee: PEP Broadsheet 532.
Other source: National Labour Market Board of Sweden Annual Report, July 1972–June 1973.

their policies a more realistic view of the behaviour of labour markets. Swedish authorities do not believe that general measures are enough in themselves. That approach is inadequate whether from the point of view of containing inflation, or as a device for shifting manpower and other resources out of the less productive sectors into the more efficient ones. For those allocative changes to be produced by the labour market, market-supportive measures are needed. And that, in the Swedish view, requires direct action from powerful institutions with large resources of finance and skilled personnel at their disposal.

A Tradition of Cyclical Fine Tuning   Like other Western European countries, Sweden too has had to contend with rising prices. But unlike the others, the Swedish authorities have not, in this period, tried to apply "incomes policy", nor have they relied wholly on fiscal and monetary policies to regulate overall demand. Although tax changes and changes in money rates have been used, these have been a part of a battery of measures. In that package of measures, increasingly more reliance has been put on direct stimulation of the working of labour markets. The trick that the Swedes have pulled off is to lower overall demand without apparently putting a great many more people out of work.

This combination of micro with macro measures for anti-inflationary purposes derives from a long Swedish tradition of sophisticated economic steering. Originally, the purpose of that complex of economic regulatory techniques was the smoothing out of cyclical fluctuations in demand. That pre-occupation is an aspect of the Swedes' deep rooted commitment to the fullest possible utilisation of the labour force. Traditionally, the Swedish authorities have preferred to "make work" for people who would be unemployed if the labour market was left to itself. Particularly because of the seasonality of outdoor work (in building and construction) caused by the severity of the Swedish climate, government support of the labour market has taken the form of public programmes of road building and other construction. Direct public programmes (planned and operated by the national manpower agency) have provided a large part of this deliberately-created labour demand. Additionally, through a scheme of Investment Reserve Funds, the authorities have attempted to stimulate private sector demand for manpower at times when the labour market is slack.

For a long time now, the Swedes have thought in direct terms about jobs, people and unemployment. Consequently, as – in common with other Western Euopean countries – Sweden has had to worry about inflation, it has adapted and modified for this purpose well-tried methods of influencing labour markets as well as developing new ones. Among these new measures is the use of a large scale adult training programme to mop up unemployment.

Though his views were more apposite to the Conservative Government's prices and incomes policy, the present Government is faced with a not dissimilar situation, with suggestions that some "muscle" be applied to the Social Contract which is *per se* an incomes policy, even though it may not be a very effective one (see Chapter 2).

It would appear that some guidance might be taken from the Swedish employment system.

Aims and Measures   Of the total Swedish labour force of some 5 million people, 7% are employed in agriculture and forestry, while mining and manufacturing account for 28% and building and construction for 9%. Commerce, transport, administration, medical and social care, services, etc. are demanding an increasing number of personnel and in the 1970s more than half of the total manpower will be employed within these sectors.

As in all other industrialised countries, the demand for manpower varies, due to economic fluctuations, although in general these variations have become smaller. It is mainly technical and structural developments and consumption which determine production and thereby the need for manpower. Old firms are closed or amalgamated, new firms are founded. As a result of progress in research, new products are created unceasingly and thereby new occupations and new work opportunities replace those which have become redundant.

The supply of manpower is also changing. There are large variations over the short-term. Sweden's labour force totals approximately 5 million, but during the course of a year about 4.5 million are on the labour market at some time. During the next decade a slight decrease is expected in the total supply of manpower. An increase is foreseen among married women, due to a higher rate of employment and to immigration, particularly from Finland.

A decrease is expected, however, in the supply of male manpower, due to a higher level of study in the lower age groups, and improved conditions of retirement.

Previously, there were labour markets with local limits. Nowadays, neither the municipality, the county nor even the country, can be considered an isolated market, as the labour market has become more and more international. Rationalisation and the concentration of firms have effects which transcend county borders and national frontiers. Therefore, contact and co-operation are necessary to solve the various problems which are caused by this development; contacts and co-operation between individuals, firms, trades, authorities and countries. This is where labour market policy has a task to fulfil. By using appropriate, selective measures it tries to facilitate the adjustment of manpower supply and demand to changed conditions. The aim is to prevent both unemployment and a manpower shortage. If the desired balance on the labour market can be attained, this will support measures in other fields to reach a balanced economy, thereby realising the aim of economic policy, which is full employment, rapid economic growth and a more uniform distribution of income in a balanced economy.

Economic developments during the last four or five years have placed great demands on labour market policy. It seems likely that these demands will remain very high compared with previous years. This is in part due to expected rapid technological and structural changes in the Swedish economy. Such a development creates special problems for certain manpower categories, e.g. persons with physical handicaps, unskilled labour, older workers, those who cannot move from their home areas, etc. If these "marginal" groups are to find employment, intensive and highly-differentiated labour market policy measures are required.

Of course, in times of recession, like the one experienced during 1972, great demands are placed on labour market policy. However, even if there is an overall balance, this does not exclude the possibility of local differences in employment opportunities within a particular occupation. There may be a manpower shortage in some places at the same time as employment opportunities are scarce in others. There exist considerable regional differences, particularly between the northern parts of the country and the rest of Sweden. Thus, according to the labour force sample surveys, the average unemployment rate in the first quarters of 1972 and 1973 was 4.0% and 4.8% respectively for the seven northernmost counties, compared with 2.4% and 2.5% for the three big-city counties and 2.5% and 2.6% for the other counties. Central and local authorities assist in restoring the balance when the employment opportunities offered by private firms are insufficient to meet the total demand for employment, and also when firms need personnel, whether for running current production or for expansion. Within the frame of a balanced labour market development, it is also necessary to meet effects arising from cyclical fluctuations. These display almost a four-year periodicity and vary in strength. Consequently, labour market policy includes measures to facilitate the levelling out of geographical and occupational disequilibria, as well as measures to support or create employment.

In periods of manpower shortage, the opportunities of obtaining employment are stepped up for such groups as married women, elderly and disabled persons: categories for whom special measures are necessary. Sometimes, re-training and further education are needed as part of an introduction to a new job.

In the case of shortage of employment opportunities, the full range of labour market policy measures becomes available to be used for each separate need: the employment service and vocational training are intensified, public relief works are increased in number, extra Government orders are given to industry, public building is speeded up, and private investments are stimulated in various ways. When the employment situation has improved, the measures to create employment became less important, but the need for an employment service and re-training always remains to satisfy the demand for manpower.

Obviously, to attain balance on the labour market is not the only aim of labour market policy. Its first aim is to assist individuals to find the kind of work which gives them maximum economic and personal satisfaction. During the 1970s an increased adjustment of work to worker is expected. Employment service, vocational guidance and vocational training represent the main implements here, but the attempts to locate firms in areas which have a manpower surplus are an important complement to the mobility-promoting policy.

In addition, great efforts are required to tackle the problem of adapting places of work and working environments to human circumstances, in order to avoid a future split on the labour market between one sector for healthy, well-educated persons and another for the handicapped and poorly-educated.

Extensive information activities must be undertaken to revise the rather widespread misconceptions about the abilities of elderly and handicapped persons. Furthermore, industry and society must adjust requirements and tasks so that this growing group of work applicants also has a chance of obtaining meaningful, productive employment in regular production.

Organisation of the Labour Market Board Immediately under the Government (Ministry of Labour and Housing), the body responsible for shaping and putting labour market policy into effect is the Labour Market Administration, i.e. the National Labour Market Board (Arbetsmarknadsstyrelsen,

AMS) with its regional agencies, the County Labour Boards (Länsarbetsnämnderna), its district agencies, the District Offices (distriktskontoren), the local Employment Offices and agents. The National Board follows development on the labour market throughout Sweden – and also abroad – and shapes current labour market policy accordingly. The main instrument here is the Employment Service, which has a widely ramified organisation. Measures are co-ordinated regionally – along the lines laid down by the National Board – by County Labour Boards, to which the District Employment Offices are attached.

The National Board's field of activity includes supervision of the public employment service, control of private employment agencies, management of vocational guidance and rehabilitation services, following up or stimulating other authorities' planning of projects suitable to be carried out as relief works, directing of the start and discontinuation of such works, management of the investment reserve system for private companies, issuing of starting permits for building, advice as to location of new industrial establishments, control of voluntary unemployment insurance funds, as well as the handling of manpower problems in time of war and applications for deferment of military service. To a great extent these functions are delegated to the regional agencies.

The Governing Body of the Board consists of a Director General who is Chairman of the Board, a Deputy Director General and eleven members appointed by the Government, three on the proposal of the Swedish Employers' Confederation (SAF), three proposed by the Confederation of Swedish Trade Unions (LO), two by the Central Organisation of Salaried Employees (TCO), and one by the Swedish Confederation of Professional Association (SACO). In addition, there is a member representing female labour and a member for agriculture.

Proposals for a new organisation of the Labour Market Board, submitted in the Administration's budget proposals for fiscal 1972/73, were approved by Parliament in the spring of 1972 and introduced with effect from 1 July 1972. Under the management of the Board there are thus three departments, one for Labour Market Services, one for Employment Planning and one for Finance and Administration. These three departments are divided in turn into sixteen divisions. In addition, there is an audit office and a press and visitors' office directly under management.

The regional agencies of the Board are the 24 County Labour Boards. These are in charge of the public employment service in each county and consist of a chairman – the Governor of the County – and seven, in some counties eight, members, representing employers' and employees' organisations. At the end of June, 1973, the employment service had 69 District Offices, 151 local offices, 32 employment service agents and 24 regional offices.

Co-operation between trade unions, employers and labour market authorities takes place both within the National Board, the County Boards, the District Offices and, locally, through continuous contacts between the employment offices and the organisations of the parties concerned. Furthermore there are local working parties for special matters, e.g. older workers, handicapped persons and building workers.

Support for the Re-adjustment and Employment of the Unemployed   Various measures have been taken to promote the readjustment and employment of the unemployed. Labour market training has been expanded and differentiated.

In accordance with the Labour Market Ordinance, transfer grants are available, under certain conditions, for unemployed persons who are unable to find a job in or near their place of residence and who must therefore move to another locality. The allowances available include travelling allowances (to seek and take up employment or for the removal of the family and the transport of household goods), a starting allowance (for expenses during the initial period in the new employment), and a separation allowance (for breadwinners who have to maintain two households). Moreover, an equipment allowance is available for families who move from areas with particularly high and persistent unemployment, to take up employment in another area.

The starting allowance is a maximum of 1,000 kronor (£105) for breadwinners and 750 kronor (£80) for others. The separation allowance, which is granted for a maximum of twelve months, is 450 kronor (£49) a month plus 100 kronor (£10) a month for every child under 16. The equipment allowance is 2,000 kronor (£210) plus 150 kronor (£15) for each child.

The Board was also entitled to grant special family allowances to providers who are hit by seasonal unemployment. This allowance, 300 kronor (£30) a month for a maximum of six months, is intended to make it easier for seasonally unemployed persons to obtain a job in another locality while waiting to return to their ordinary work in their home district.

The Board was also able to grant rent allowances on an experimental basis to workers who had to move, up to a maximum of twelve months. The rent allowance is intended to ease the transitional increase in housing costs that usually accompanies a move.

Transfer grants may also be provided for "key personnel" taking up employment with regional development firms.

The Labour Market Board was authorised in 1965, in consultation with the National Housing Board, to support owner-occupiers by buying their homes when they are forced to move because of unemployment. The activity covers the four northernmost counties but can be extended to other parts of the country if special circumstances render this desirable. Property that can be bought through the agricultural fund cannot be purchased under the above rules.

Labour market training has been provided in order to solve the adjustment problems of the individuals as well as to satisfy the demand for trained labour. Such training has been available for persons aged 20 or more who have been, or are in danger of becoming, unemployed, or who are difficult to place on the labour market, provided the training is considered necessary as a means of obtaining permanent employment.

In July 1972, 36,124 persons were taking part in labour market training schemes, 13,768 of them are women. 106,697 persons started training during the year; of these 51,246 were women. 142,821 persons in all thus took part in labour market training schemes in the 1972/3 fiscal year, of whom 65,014 were women. The corresponding figure for the preceding year was 130,693 persons, of whom 58,195 were women.

For unemployed persons who obtained employment in new, converted or expanded enterprises in parts of the country belonging to the development area, training was arranged within the framework of industrial location policy. The training followed curricula adopted by the employer and employee organisations concerned. The trainees were paid ordinary wages and the enterprise received a grant towards the costs of training from the Labour Market Board.

During the year, a special training grant of Skr 5 per trainee per hour has been payable to firms, in addition to their normal recruitment, hiring and training youths under 25 and women. If special reasons existed, this grant could also be paid for men over 25. Through this measure about 5,200 persons, of whom some 4,300 youths, obtained employment and training during the year.

The increase in unemployment during the autumn of 1972 was met in part by expanding employment on relief work. This was facilitated, e.g. by the government grant for municipal relief work being increased to 75%. An average of 33,000 persons a month were employed in this way during the year compared with 31,000 the previous fiscal year. The number employed on general relief work decreased by 3,000 persons, while an increase by 5,000 persons was noted for special relief projects, which are intended for those with special handicaps as well as for elderly workers with local ties. In April, 1973 a total of 48,000 persons, 6,600 of them women, were engaged on some kind of relief work. Special measures were taken to provide work for unemployed young people and in April 1973 some 12,000 or 26% of those on relief work were under 25 years old.

Relief work has taken the form of road-work, water supplies

and drainage, house building, forestry, nature conservancy, cultural projects, office work, inquiry work, technical work, nursing and service work. Industrial relief work, which was introduced in 1966, is intended for persons who are difficult to place when communities with insufficient job opportunities are hit by unemployment. The projects consist in the manufacture of industrial products.

For a long time now, certain groups in sparsely-populated areas have been especially exposed to unemployment. They are chiefly elderly persons who used to earn a living in forestry, agriculture, construction work, e.g. for hydroelectric schemes, or service occupations.

Projects for relief work have been selected to coincide as far as possible with the composition and previous occupational experience of the labour involved.

Bibliography

Scotland's Goals: Fourth International Forum of the Scottish Council (Development & Industry) *Jack McGill Collins £6.50*

Structure and Growth of the Scottish Economy *T. L. Johnston, N. K. Buxton, D. Mair Collins £3.25*

Scotland and Unemployment *Santosh Mukherjee Scottish International Education Trust £1.50*

Making Labour Markets Work *Santosh Mukherjee PEP Broadsheet 532 £2*

Oil and World Power: Background to the Oil Crisis *Peter R. Odell Penguin £0.60*

Fairfields: A Study of Industrial Change *Kenneth J. W. Alexander and C. L. Jenkins Allan Lane Press £2.50*

Crisis on the Clyde *Jack McGill Davis-Poynter £2.50*

Index